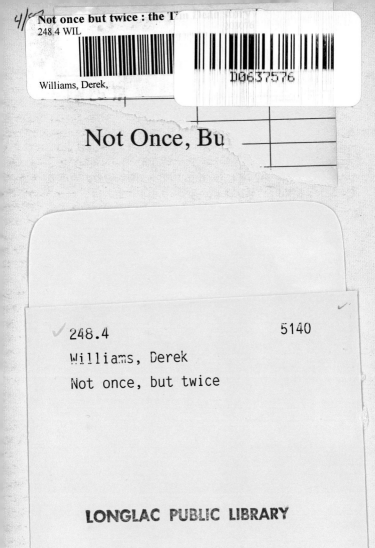

Not Once, Bu

By the same author

About People *(IVP)*
Pocket Handbook of Christian Living *(Scripture Union)*
One in a Million *(Word Books)*

Not Once, But Twice
The Tim Dean Story
Derek Williams

HODDER AND STOUGHTON
LONDON SYDNEY AUCKLAND TORONTO

British Library Cataloguing in Publication Data

Dean, Tim
   Not once but twice : the Tim Dean story.
   1. Christian life——1960–
   I. Title   II. Williams, Derek, *1945*–
   248.4   BV4501.2

   ISBN 0-340-38342-9

For Margaret

Who watched and waited

Preface

I never read long introductions to books, and therefore do not intend to write one; I have always felt that any book which requires a detailed explanation before it gets under way is somewhat deficient.

However, one declaration of interest may help you. The subject of this book is Tim Dean, and especially the near-fatal illnesses he has suffered. He and I are more than ships passing in the night. We have, on several occasions, worked together. Like Alfred Hitchcock, the horror film director, I therefore have a habit of appearing in the story in some minor role, a fact which also explains why I have occasionally adopted the technique of St Luke, the author of the *Acts of the Apostles*, and inserted otherwise unexplained 'we' passages. The pronoun 'I' only occurs within quotation marks and, when unattributed, always refers to Tim himself.

Apart from that, what follows is Tim's story told as dispassionately as is possible in the circumstances, placing his at times horrendous sufferings in their proper context of a varied and colourful life and a significant period of recent history. Where we disagree on detailed points of Christian understanding, I have stuck to his views; where we agree I have sometimes taken the liberty of expanding on his ideas and even adding one or two of my own, to reinforce the point he wishes to make. I defy future generations of source critics to disentangle the threads.

True to form, as something of a perfectionist, Tim has insisted that a number of facts be checked by others and that members of his family and close friends be persuaded to talk frankly about his weaknesses as well as his strengths. Our joint thanks go to those who patiently raked through their memories on our behalf. Thanks, too, to Dr Gillian Vaughan Hudson, who appears in the narrative and who has kindly checked the medical details; to Catherine Rawlings for some dusty delving into my library for every conceivable reference to the mystery of suffering with which to prime my thoughts and to check Tim's; to Pat and Beryl Goodland for providing a quiet retreat where nesting starlings outside the window somehow stimulated the Muse; and to my wife Susan for typing many more words than eventually reached the final draft, after tiring days caring for three small children.

No book on the subject of suffering – and especially nothing more than a reflective biography such as this – can hope to solve all the problems it raises. Each person's perception and experience demands a unique answer. But we can expect some illumination in a world which the Christian claims has been invaded by 'the Light of the world', Jesus Christ, who himself underwent intense, unimaginable suffering.

Our hope is that Tim's story in *Not Once But Twice* will be a means of chasing away a few of the shadows. And even, perhaps, of making you smile.

Derek Williams
Wiltshire
Spring 1986

Contents

Only once or twice in life is it permitted to a man to see the very universe from outside, and to feel existence itself as an adorable adventure not yet begun.

G. K. Chesterton

The only one worth listening to is he who has himself suffered.

Lord Coggan

One

To hell and back – with love

'Statistically, I shouldn't live very long. But I've rubbished the statistics for so many years that maybe there's hope!'

Tim Dean talks about his prospects of life and death with as much ease as most of us talk about the weather. Words roll easily off the tongue of this tall, slim man in his mid-thirties. He uses his hands and slender fingers expressively as he speaks with gentle earnestness, not about theories but about his own vivid and traumatic experiences.

'I've been through the nearest thing I can imagine to hell. I don't want to go through it again. And I wouldn't wish it on my worst enemy.'

But those are not words of bitterness. 'I remember sitting in hospital one night, about midnight, when most of the lights were out, and looking round at the other men in the ward. I knew them pretty well, and the tremendous afflictions they had. Curiously, I felt I was privileged to be there and to suffer alongside these people. I don't believe in the sanctity of suffering, but there is a sense of privilege to being alongside people as a co-sufferer. I'm still trying to take on board what the piece of illumination I received that night really means.'

At home with his wife Margaret, in their 1930s semi-detached house in a quiet cul-de-sac in Guildford, thirty miles south-west of central London, Tim betrays no signs of having suffered. He is casually but neatly dressed with a tie and high-necked jumper; his mousy hair and gingery beard are trim. Behind his gold-rimmed glasses are alert hazel eyes, which can dart from person to person, or hold one with strong, unwavering attention.

Yet there have been occasions in his comparatively short life – just half the traditional span of three score years and ten – when he has been reduced to a sack of skin and bone. He has been seared with intense pains, and pitched into the dark nights of blind depression. Powerful drugs – one of them derived from an old wartime poison gas – have made his hair and beard fall out and his eyes glaze over, and have reduced his normally fluent speech to a mumbled slur, his confident stride to the shuffle of an old man.

Tim Dean has had two rare forms of cancer, with a dozen years separating them. He was not expected to survive either. On both occasions, he and his medical advisers were standing at the frontiers of human knowledge. At a late point in his story there was only one other known case in Britain identical to his, and hence no medical experience of how to treat him.

Not once but twice, he has seen his life threatened by a malign sickness. He has twice peered over the edge of the abyss into the unknown depths of the grave; he has twice surrendered himself into the hands of his maker, aware that the final curtain could fall on his earthly life at any moment.

Yet each time he has been pulled back from the brink by an unseen hand which he recognises as God's. He has received his life back in circumstances which have always been remarkable; at times almost unbelievable.

Talk to his friends, even to Margaret his wife, and they will tell you that Tim has not changed much over the years. He has a determined streak; you can see it in his positive stride, hear it in his emphatic speech. He is one of those people with a knack of making things happen, of never taking no for an answer. It is partly a family trait, but it has also been born partly of circumstances. Life has never been easy for him; one ageing relative always prefaces her comments about him with 'Poor Tim!' Time and again, he has found himself in at the deep end, where sink or swim have been the only alternatives.

And he has more recently been at the sharp end, too,

where big issues are debated, policies formed and decisions executed. As the editor of the Christian monthly *Third Way* he rubs shoulders with politicians, media personalities and church leaders. Some of them make brief appearances in these pages, alongside others whose names may ring no bells but who have played equally significant supporting roles in his saga.

But see him in his garden, as he picks up and strokes his pet Dutch rabbits Rockall and Bailey, potentially vicious creatures which would kill each other if they were not permanently separated by wire netting. Or observe him indoors, cooking some exotic dish or happily ironing the week's washload (shared roles are the rule for Tim and Margaret), then pausing to watch a siskin or chaffinch through the window. And notice him talking naturally to the young children of his friends and close relatives, some of them very fond of their uncle Tim.

Then you will see a streak of tenderness to lay alongside the determination, a love for the weaker, smaller things of life, as well as a passionate concern for the big issues and deep questions. A compulsive talker, he has learnt to listen more. A vigorous activist, he has rediscovered the joy of simply being a unique person in a colourful world. Above all, through his painful, turbulent illnesses he has seen the perspective of human existence in sharper focus than many who may use the same words and share the same beliefs.

He often quotes St Paul to encapsulate the truths he has discovered:

Christ is the image of the Invisible God, the firstborn over all creation. For by him all things were created: things in heaven and on earth, visible and invisible, whether thrones or powers or rulers or authorities; all things were created by him and for him. He is before all things, and in him all things hold together. And he is the head of the body, the church; he is the beginning and the firstborn from among the dead, so that in everything he might have the supremacy. For God was pleased to have

all his fulness dwell in him, and through him to reconcile
to himself all things, whether things on earth or things in
heaven, by making peace through his blood, shed on the
cross (Col.1: 15–20).

During his second illness, Tim realised afresh that earthly,
temporal life is as much about Jesus Christ as heavenly,
eternal life. 'Why is it meaningful to prune roses or make a
painting? If there's no Christ, it's meaningless, vanity,
chasing after wind. Everything – including politics, art,
ecology – has a meaning in Christ. Everything ultimately
exists for him. We answer to someone outside ourselves;
when we become egocentric we're lost.'

And he discovered anew what that means to the individual. 'You are never more alone than in the middle of
suffering. But there was one particular moment in hospital
when I suddenly felt very close to Christ, and I understood
more of what it means to feel love for him. Loving Christ is
inextricably bound up with serving and obeying him; for he
said, "If you love me, you will obey what I command"
(John 14:15). But what I feel is also part of it.

'Purely and simply – and profoundly – the Christian
difference in suffering is that Jesus is with the sufferer in a
very real way. And that's been my experience.'

The experience is past but the lessons remain for the
present and the uncertain future. For the time being Tim
has indeed rubbished the medical statistics and lived to tell
a tale of how faith, hope and love can abide in the midst of
pain, fear and grief. And in that, at least, he has also proved
one of his school teachers wrong.

'Dean!' he was once told, 'you'll never make anything
out of your life.'

He always was the odd one out.

Two

The die is cast

'I was a little weed, a sensitive kid who was easily upset. I had a short back and sides, wore health service glasses and was totally non-athletic. It meant I was picked on.'

He was also the youngest of three children – Tony was seven years his senior and Verity four – which meant the young Tim tended to be left out of things at home, too. And, added to that, their father Len worked night shifts at London's Heathrow Airport as a storekeeper. His absence during the week put a degree of strain on the family. Home life was always strict, and punishments for misbehaviour were often saved up by their mother, Joan, until their father was around at the weekend.

Tim was born on Tuesday the thirteenth of June 1950, a fact which, despite his later traumas, has never tempted him to become superstitious; his positive Christian faith excludes such fatalism. The happy event took place at a nursing home on the south coast of England, much to Tim's later regret. It was far from the family home by Ham Park in London's East End. To have been born at home would have entitled him to be called a true Cockney, with all the pride of the East End community that involves. He made up for this accident of birth by following the family tradition of supporting West Ham United soccer club, a passion which began at an early age and which he retains to the present day. His grandfather had been a keen supporter; his father recalls being on the terraces at the Upton Park stadium on the day when the first daylight air raid was launched on London in World War II. The game was stopped and everyone gazed up at the German planes overhead.

As soon as Tim was old enough, in his early teens, he often trekked back across London (the family having moved westwards), nourished by a flask of cold drinking chocolate and some sandwiches, to watch West Ham's home games. When he was fifteen he went with his father to sample the exhilarating atmosphere of 80,000 people packing Wembley Stadium, singing West Ham's song, 'I'm forever blowing bubbles', and watching their team beat TSV Munich 2–0 in the 1965 European Cup Winners Cup Final.

The family had migrated to the south-western side of London when Tim was only two. They went to live on a housing estate at Bedfont, within walking distance of the southern perimeter of Heathrow. 'I can still remember the wonderful sound of propeller aircraft revving up.' Avro Yorks, DC6s and Elizabethans caught the imagination of the young Tim. He found more pleasure in watching the planes from the school window than in doing his lessons. His mind drifted to the skies; the wanderlust was awakened within him and has never subsided; geography became his favourite subject, and he developed an enduring fascination for maps and landscapes. In the school dining room at lunch time the other children fuelled Tim's interest by competing to see who could first identify approaching planes and the airlines they belonged to.

Car owners were such a rarity on the lower middle-class estate that the children could play cricket against the street lampposts without fear of being run down or of damaging vehicles. Even compared with their neighbours, the Deans were not well off and had to struggle to make ends meet. But the 1950s were boom time in Britain, and when at the start of the next decade Prime Minister Harold Macmillan uttered his famous dictum, 'You've never had it so good', Len Dean agreed. He then had a rather battered Morris 8 car to prove it.

Tim was still at infant school when he said to his mother

one morning, 'Mum, you'll have to go to the shop and buy me some glasses, because I can't see properly.' He was found to be short-sighted and today can only focus unaided on things which are a few inches from his eyes. He also had his first experience of hospital at this time. He fell and split his right eyebrow open, and was taken to a casualty department. The local anaesthetic did not work and he was screaming loudly as the doctor stitched him up. 'That didn't endear hospitals to me very much.'

A couple of years later, when he was about eight, Tim went into hospital to have his adenoids removed. He was given a drug in a purple liquid and told it was blackcurrant juice; it tasted foul and it was some years before he would look at blackcurrant juice again. The boy in the next bed was presented with a large model aircraft carrier; Tim's family could afford no such gifts. The incident provided him with an early emotional introduction to the issue of social equality and justice; he was later to find it illuminated and intensified by Christianity.

Tony and Verity were both academically bright and sailed through their Eleven-Plus exams to go to grammar school, the top stream in the state education system of the day. Tim's parents expected him to follow the same path, but he was a slow developer and not particularly interested in school work. He did scrape through the exam, but that led him to two of the unhappiest years of his life.

Eleven years old, he entered Isleworth Grammar School. He hated every minute of it; to him it was cold, unwelcoming and at times fearsome. In the playground might was right and stronger children bullied him. The teachers in their academic gowns seemed distant and inhuman. They urged him to try harder but their pleas fell on deaf ears. He came bottom in almost every subject.

On the last day of term Len Dean went in to see the headmaster, leaving his son sitting in the corridor outside, and announced that he was taking him away from the school immediately. Tim had no chance to say goodbye to the few friends he had made; lessons were over and the school was deserted.

Fortuitously – and it is one of many coincidences which shine like breaks in the cloud in Tim's story and which give added credibility to his firm belief in God's kingship over human life – a girl who lived near the Deans went to the now demolished Woodfield Secondary Modern School. She was always saying how good it was, and Tim decided he would like to go there too. He did not live within its official catchment area, but the system bent sufficiently to allow the transfer.

It was like entering an oasis after a journey across the desert. The atmosphere was friendly and relaxed. He was put into a class which went on to attain a higher rate of General Certificate O-level passes than the academically superior school he had left. He discovered that the children respected achievement whether it was athletic or academic; the tough ones were often also the brightest. With the crude logic of a thirteen year old adolescent, he soon realised that if he wanted to be accepted by his peers he had to work hard and come top of the class. Within a year he was regularly rated third or fourth out of some thirty children.

He also had a Christian teacher, Mr Mayo. 'And this guy cared. He astounded me. He said, "If there's anything you can't do or understand, come out and ask. I don't care if I'm here after school till five o'clock helping you so long as you work." I thought it couldn't be true so I took him at his word and tested him out. I found he was really nice. He had a genuine concern for the pupils.'

Good teachers cannot do the student's work, of course, and while the atmosphere was more congenial Tim still preferred to daydream. He was – and in some respects still is – a person who needs strong motivation before doing anything. At home he always enjoyed drawing, for example, and was fascinated by detail, but usually he needed to be told what to draw by his mother. He loved discovering new interests, and he enjoyed practical things like making up plastic aircraft kits. At school maths bored him silly until he began algebra, logarithms and calculus. Suddenly the subject became creative and conceptual, almost a game in which numbers turn into building blocks, and it came alive for him.

When he did see a good purpose in doing something, he threw himself into it heart and soul. The family memory banks are filled with stories of his adolescent obsessions. Collecting bus registration numbers was one brief but intense passion. When he could afford it he bought a Rover ticket and toured London Transport depots, recording the vehicle numbers in notebooks and on scraps of paper which he then left around the neat little house.

Later in his teens he became addicted to a forerunner of TV satirical programmes, *At Last the 1948 Show*, which starred John Cleese, whose fame was to be sealed by *Monty Python* and *Fawlty Towers*. While working temporarily at Heathrow one vacation he met and talked with Cleese, who was passing through the airport. For weeks after his brief encounter he talked of little but his good friend John 'Otto' Cleese.

But nothing is wasted in this life, it seems. In retrospect, his single-minded passions, his curiosity and attention to detail were being flexed and strengthened in childhood and teen years. There was to come a time when, as a young man in the clutches of a potentially fatal disease, he would draw on those very qualities in order to survive.

By the summer of 1966, the sixteen year old Tim was beginning to discover the personal confidence which had previously eluded him. That was the time of England's historic and nail-biting World Cup Final victory over West Germany, and soccer was high on the schoolboy agenda. Although he was not physically strong, Tim's sporting prowess was increasing. He thought about his game and tried to develop the skills he needed to compensate for what he lacked physically. He went into the sixth form for the 1966–67 school year, to complete his O-levels, and spent a lot of the time kicking a ball; he played for a sixth form eleven against the school side and scored three goals, to give his team a surprise victory.

He was a prefect by then, too, sharing in the basic organising and discipline of the school. He saw others being victimised as he had once been, and rather than turn a blind eye to bullying in the usual tradition of the blackboard jungle, he did what he could to put a stop to it.

His organisational skills came into their own one wintry day when the whole school took on the fourteen prefects in a snowball fight. Basing his strategy on the closing scenes of the film *Zulu*, he divided his Gideon's army into two ranks, each rank in turn slinging its snowballs in a volley; two girl prefects were deputed to supply the rest with ammunition. They held their ranks, preserved their honour and for the first time in the school's history the prefects were not routed!

After school there were frequent parties in each other's homes, where they danced to the music of the Rolling Stones and the Beach Boys. Those were civilised times; there were small quantities of alcohol at the parties but no drugs, and at one o'clock in the morning Tim could walk home alone, pausing to talk to the donkeys which grazed in a roadside meadow.

He was usually one of the last to leave, because he invariably became involved in the serious discussions which began when the dancers tired. In the inevitable teenage mix of broad generalisations and wild assertions, he felt that Christianity was given a raw deal. 'I had already become convinced of the truth of Christianity but I would never have called myself a Christian. So I found myself putting forward the Christian case, although I made it quite clear that I was not there. I felt that they were sometimes unfair to Christianity and that the case had to be answered.'

Those discussions gradually clarified his beliefs and so played a vital role in Tim's ultimate commitment to Jesus Christ, and his personal acceptance of the faith which had always been part of his home life. His parents had been churchgoers whose faith had come alive shortly after they moved to Bedfont. To the children, the only observable difference was that their father gave up smoking and stopped doing what seemed perfectly natural to him – going to church and calling in at the pub on the way home – because some of the church elders found the habit offensive. He drank his beer at home instead. During the 1954 Billy Graham crusade at Harringay Arena, their mother, Joan, sang in the massed choir.

The local church – Hatton Road Baptist – was a plain brick and corrugated asbestos building, which held little attraction for the Dean children. The only compensation for Tim was that there, as at his junior school, he could look through the window and see the aircraft landing at Heathrow. The worship was formal and the teaching dry, making the faith it espoused unattractive and dull for teenagers who were then discovering the delights of rock 'n' roll. There was a marginally brighter and influential young people's Christian Endeavour group, which encouraged its members to take an active part in meetings by reading, speaking or praying aloud, and Tim became involved in this until he was old enough to withstand parental pressure to attend, and could distance himself from the church.

But the seeds of faith had been sown in his mind, and they lay dormant for a while until a new minister arrived at the church. Eric Willett, who later became a missionary in Peru, was a young ex-RAF photographer. One of his innovations was to start a youth coffee bar and organise gospel pop concerts. The informal atmosphere said as much as – or more than – the words of the singers and speakers: it was culturally relevant, and showed that Christianity need not be buried in the traditions of one generation and thus alienate the next.

Tim was drawn in to the preparations for a gospel concert in the summer of 1967; he made some posters to publicise the event. He was deeply impressed by Mike Keen, the evangelist, and he went on to the Sunday evening after-church meeting at a nearby house. He had been quietly thinking things out for a while, and as they talked through

the implications of Christianity, he said publicly, 'I've become a Christian.' It was much more than an intellectual
assent to the creeds; it was a characteristic heart and soul
decision to accept Christ personally and to put him first in
his life – Tim never does things half-heartedly.

'I was challenged to get up and follow Christ. I knew
what I was doing; there was no blind faith as such. I knew
that Jesus's death on the cross was the only solution for
humanity that made sense.' The point of commitment, it
seemed, was the moment he opened his mouth, a dynamic
example of St Paul's assertion that 'it is with your heart that
you believe and are justified, and it is with your mouth that
you confess and are saved' (Rom. 10:10). It was quite an
event; half a dozen others in the group also became
Christians about the same time.

As he returned home that night, his sister Verity met him
coming up the path. He threw his arms round her and said,
'It's all changed. I understand it all now. I've given my life
to the Lord.' Tim had been captivated by Christ. His commitment was not an endorsement of his church, which he
still found irritating at times, but he did begin attending it
regularly again, and was later baptised.

The little weed had grown up, and had discovered that he
was not despised by his maker, and that he was even
accepted by other people. The die had been cast; the rough
shape of his personality was sketched out.

Then, three weeks after his conversion to Christ, he had
a rude awakening.

Three

Culture shock

Tim had enrolled at Ealing Art College. On the first day of term in September 1967 he arrived wearing a jacket and grey flannel trousers, his hair short and trim. All the other students turned up in an assortment of denims and un-orthodox gear, their hair generally long and untidy.

He was given a questionnaire to fill in. One question asked: *Are you promiscuous?* He had never come across the word before, and wisely answered no.

It was not long before he discovered its meaning; Janice, a girl in his group, illustrated it perfectly. She too had been at Bedfont Infants School, although Tim had not seen her since. Travelling across London one day to a party with a group of students, she accepted a dare and wore only a short fur coat, with nothing underneath. She dressed in the ladies room at a station, but once the party was under way soon found herself in bed with one of the men present.

The sexual and cultural revolution was at its height at this time. Students were having sexual relationships with their tutors. It was the era of hippies and 'happenings'; John Lennon of the Beatles and Yoko Ono made one of their famous protest gestures for peace at the *Alchemical Wedding* at the Royal Albert Hall in London. They appeared on stage and rolled around it in a bag, to the mixed applause and bewilderment of the audience, which included Tim and some of his friends.

For the eighteen year old Tim, art college came as his second culture shock within a month. He had only just made his Christian commitment, and he had firmly accepted biblical standards of morality. He was in the honeymoon period of discovering a new spiritual dynamic; it was not in his character to be half-hearted about the faith he had so recently embraced. And suddenly he had found himself in this strange world-within-the-world that he had not known existed.

In his first tutorial, he was asked why he had come to art college. Tim said that he really wanted to make films, but did not know how to; going to art college seemed as good a way as any to find out. Even then, at the back of his mind there lay a desire to make good Christian films. He had seen some films at Hatton Road Baptist Church, and had wondered why they were shot and structured so appallingly, in comparison with the professional offerings on show at the cinema.

As his time at Woodfield School had drawn to a close, he had been faced with the perennial question as to what to do next. Unemployment was not high at the time, and theoretically he could have left the education system and found a job. But he had eight O-level passes (plus two O-level equivalent passes in additional subjects in the academically lower-grade CSE syllabus), as well as a fertile and creative mind, and he would not have been suited to an unskilled job. He did once spend a vacation working on the assembly line at the Champion Spark Plug factory, and found it 'boring and abysmal'. The people on the production line had become extensions to the machines; they ignored their automatic physical movements and talked and sang all day.

Tim had only one obvious talent and interest, although even that did not rate among his obsessions. He could draw a little, and he enjoyed doing it. The youth employment officer, when he discovered the fact, rather offhandedly said, 'Well, you'd better try art school then.' So he did, with his father's blessing. Len Dean had seen his two elder children go on to higher things, Tony becoming a metallurgist and Verity a social worker, but he was wise enough to allow his youngest son to do what he wanted, even though he had reservations on the subject. The question 'what do you do next?' was obviously going to arise again in a few years' time, and the answer would be hard to find.

Never one to enjoy being the odd one out, Tim grew his hair until it reached his shoulders. It led to a head-on confrontation with his father, who had promised to take Tim on a trip to Hong Kong in 1968 – on condition that he had his hair cut. Tim complied, but when the order came to also shorten his sideburns, he resolutely refused. He felt he had done enough to conform, and so he forfeited an early chance of fulfilling his wanderlust. It was a mystery to him why long hair should be so controversial; all the pictures he had seen of Jesus portrayed him with long hair, so it could hardly be wrong!

He remained clean-shaven until 1969, actually enjoying the experience of shaving. Friends suggested his rather gaunt features would look better covered with a beard, so he grew one, liked it and retained it ever after – except for one brief period when he developed a skin complaint. His early beard was bushy and long; one friend described him as looking like 'a cross between Rasputin and Alan Ginsberg'. Both hair and beard were to have their unique roles to play in his first illness.

But if he conformed to the art college culture in appearance, he did not conform to its lack of moral and spiritual values. He was still the enthusiast, and he made no secret of the fact that he was a Christian. Which made one of his fellow students very uncomfortable.

Malcolm Doney was already a student on the same 'foundation' course, and a Christian. On the Friday before term began, Malcolm went with a group from his church, Wellington Hall in Hounslow, to lead a meeting at a nearby church in Feltham, during which he spoke publicly about his Christian faith. The young people from Tim's church were also there. Malcolm's heart sank, and Tim's leapt, when they discovered that they would be at Ealing together. Malcolm preferred to keep his faith quieter at college; besides, the conventional Tim looked as if he would be a misfit among bohemian students.

Tim was much more direct at the time. He was someone
who loved an argument and would often open up the conversation in an almost confrontational manner. Since that
time, he has become far less brusque, but it is still remarkably easy to find that a conversation about rabbits has
slipped unnoticed into a discussion about current government policies, or the latest religious bandwagon. As a
student he took his art college friends along to the coffee
bars and pop concerts held at the church in Bedfont, which
he began helping to organise soon after his conversion.
Bedfont had never seen such strange people before.

This, too, was the period of his obsession with *At last the
1948 Show*. And in common with many of his generation,
including Prince Charles, he was also a fanatical follower of
The Goon Show series on radio. To Malcolm it often
seemed that when Tim was not talking excitedly about
Christianity he was re-enacting, complete with passable
imitations of the unique Goon voices of Neddy Seagoon,
Bluebottle, Eccles, *et al*, the entire script of the latest
episode.

Soccer, of course, was never far from his mind, and when
the junior school next door to the art college was closed for
half-term holidays, the students used their playground to
kick a ball around in. The nineteenth century buildings
were partially supported above ground level over the playground by cast-iron girders. On one occasion, when Tim
went to head the ball, he crashed into a girder. His glasses
parted neatly in the middle and blood trickled down his
face. The Dean stiff upper lip came to the rescue; he got up
and walked slowly from the playground with the words,
'Carry on without me, lads!'

On another occasion the same highly developed streak of
seriousness erupted negatively during an end of term game
of Monopoly, for which the students had themselves drawn
the board and made the pieces. The object of the game
being to bankrupt the other players and build one's own
property empire. Tim was incensed when a tutor gave

Malcolm some of his money so that he could continue playing for a while. Tim argued fiercely that it was against the rules to bail out a bankrupt player. When no one relented, he stalked out and took no further part in the game.

When the academic year ended in July 1968, Tim and Malcolm Doney parted company. Malcolm transferred to St Martin's School of Art in central London to study fine art, while Tim remained at Ealing, to begin a graphic design course.

By this time their uneasy relationship had grown into a friendship, and they were destined to be together a great deal in the future, especially when Tim first fell ill.

Before that occurred, they were to share in something which not only profoundly shaped their thinking; it also helped to trigger a significant change of attitude in a whole section of the Christian Church.

Four

Art for God's sake

Meryl Fergus was facing a new challenge. She was a travelling secretary with the Inter-Varsity Fellowship (later re-named the Universities and Colleges Christian Fellowship), concentrating on the technical and further education colleges at the bottom end of the academic spectrum in London and the south-east of England. Her role was to support and encourage the often tiny student-led Christian Unions in such places.

From time to time she also heard of Christians in the art colleges, but they were generally too few in number to form CUs. She knew they faced problems unique to the arts world, and wanted to help them. So in 1968 she began inviting them to meet regularly to study the Bible, pray, and discuss how their work and art related to their Christian faith.

They were almost like pioneers; they certainly felt like it. It seemed that the old pharisaical restraints which had frozen some parts of Christendom into a cultural ice floe for centuries were melting at last. Once, the theatre had been synonymous with immorality; fine art was not regarded as a useful vocation. But now it was no longer so obviously wrong to put your Christian daughter on the stage – especially when you read of the bizarre acted parables put on by the Old Testament prophets. Looking in their Bibles anew, Christians were finding a God who directed the design and decoration of ancient tabernacles and temples, a creator who stamped beauty on the face of the earth, and they wanted to use their creative talents to plan and paint too.

But where would your daughter find sympathetic and spiritual help to cope with the moral and practical pressures of drama school? And when a Christian set up his easel and mixed his paints, should he then turn his back on the nude model sitting on a cushioned table in the middle of the college studio and paint instead the daffodils in the gardens outside?

They might sometimes look weird. They might sometimes behave wildly. But some art students believed in Jesus Christ. They wanted to honour him in their arts. And their questions demanded serious, thoughtful, biblical answers stripped of the clichés and false Victorian values which had contributed to the Church's cultural ice age.

Meryl Fergus gave what help she could, but her own knowledge of the arts was limited. With the encouragement of senior IVF staff, she organised a weekend conference and invited a then unknown Dutch professor to cross the North Sea and address the gathering. It proved to be the start of something big.

She scoured Britain for a conference centre which would welcome unkempt art students and allow those who wished to smoke to do so. She found The Gaynes, in the Midlands. Inside, it was painted a rather sickly green, and the roof leaked. She had no idea how many people would come. But late one Friday afternoon in November 1968 she looked down the narrow country lane and saw 'the glorious vision' of young people struggling along, rucksacks on their backs, paintings in their arms. Once inside, they began hammering their paintings onto the walls, but that was forgivable in the circumstances: they had *come*!

Among them was Tim Dean. His sister Verity, then a social science student at a technical college near the old Dean family home in West Ham, had heard about the conference from Meryl on one of the travelling secretary's regular visits to the Christian Union, and had asked for a brochure to give to Tim.

Another participant was Malcolm Doney. He was going through something of a crisis of faith at St Martin's, knowing what he believed but not why he believed it. He had been encouraged to write to the IVF office to see if they knew of other Christians at the college. They had no names to give him, but they did send a brochure for The Gaynes.

And the Dutch speaker was Hans Rookmaaker, Professor of the History of Art at the Free University of Amsterdam. Several people had almost identical first impressions of him, Tim included: 'He seemed the biggest jerk I'd ever met.' His appearance hardly helped. Rookmaaker was short and dumpy, almost pear-shaped. He wore baggy trousers and smoked a pipe. He reminded one person of the hobbits in Tolkein's fantasies. But from the moment he began to lecture in his fluent but heavily accented English on 'Three steps to modern art', he unfolded a vision of reality which many of those present were groping towards.

Tim's initial negative reaction arose partly because Rookmaaker challenged both his Christian presuppositions and his attitudes to art. Tim had been brought up in a Christian tradition which did not generally relate theology to the secular world, and up to that point he had considered that his main function as a Christian in a college was simply to witness and to evangelise. Rookmaaker stressed that Christianity had a part to play in the critique and evaluation of art, and that it should inform every area of a person's life. Tim slowly began to see the truth of that – 'I was ripe for that message' – and it was to become a firm foundation for his life and work.

The Dutchman also challenged his attitude to the modern art he liked and enjoyed. Tim still stresses that 'there is fun and joy in modern art', but Professor Rookmaaker probed beneath its surface. In his seminal book, based partly on these and other lectures in Britain, he warned:

This art is the work of your neighbours, your contemporaries, human beings who are crying out in despair for the loss of their humanity, their values, their lost absolutes, groping in the dark for answers. It is already late, if not too late, but if we want to help them our generation must hear their cry. We must listen to them as they cry out from their prison, a prison of a universe which is aimless, meaningless, absurd.[1]

It probably did not help Tim's impressions when Rookmaaker strongly criticised a huge life-size painting Tim had brought with him to the conference; it was a picture of an actress, Suzy Kendal, and he had done it with cans of spray paint.

But there was something about the man that earned his deep respect. Late one evening at The Gaynes a group sat around the fireplace with him, and Tim, bold as ever, raised the controversial subject of the Christian attitude to war. Although he had been born five years after the second world war had ended, there were often reminders of it in parental conversations at home. He could remember the ration books stacked on the sideboard when he was a young child, and his wide-ranging reading had included serious histories and accounts of the war. Human suffering was already on his mind.

Rookmaaker's answer surprised Tim. He admitted that there could be a good case for Christians in both Germany and England joining their respective armed forces – *and* for Christians in both countries abstaining altogether. He turned the ethical issue into a very human one.

'He had a breadth of vision of what Christianity meant that I'd never come across before. He exuded a whole, total philosophy of life. He could talk about science and art in a way that affirmed God as creator and brought everything within God's concern. He was concerned about individuals too. He spent time with you. He had a good fireside manner.'

Within a few years, Tim's negative reactions were to be changed into largely positive and appreciative ones. When it later fell to Tim to organise Rookmaaker's British tours, there grew between them a warmth and closeness that others envied, and which Rookmaaker expressed in typical Dutch-uncle fashion by presenting Tim with an occasional bottle of top quality Glenfiddich whisky. Rookmaaker went to his early and untimely grave, blissfully unaware that his young English travelling companion, while no tee-totaller, had little taste for the hard stuff.

But through his book and his lectures the Dutchman, often working with his close friend Francis Schaeffer in Switzerland, with whom Rookmaaker was closely associated, did far more than make the arts respectable. He introduced a whole new way of looking at the world through the windows of scripture, and provided the groundwork for the host of new organisations, pressure groups, and publications devoted to exploring a biblical perspective to contemporary issues which sprang up in the 1970s.

Tim Dean was one of his spiritual beneficiaries. Yet for the student from Ealing the most valuable result of that first of many arts students' conferences was that like-minded people from around Britain made contact with each other. None had realised so many others existed; most had thought themselves isolated pioneers. In the flush of excitement, friendships were established which lasted for years and which, in some cases, still have not been forgotten or relinquished – even though the people concerned were scattered across the country and have since moved on to varied fields of work.

Tim and Malcolm joined the London arts students Bible study group, and its venue quickly became too small to accommodate the twenty or thirty people who turned up each week. It moved to the home of Johnny Walford, an art dealer and later a student of Rookmaaker in Holland, until the Arts Centre Group was opened in Kensington in 1971, specifically as a meeting place for groups of Christians working professionally or studying in the arts world.

The two students also moved into an apartment together

in Muswell Hill Road, a short walk from Hampstead Heath, a broad green oasis set in the urban sprawl of north London. With them went David Davis and Martin Adams, who were later replaced by Tony Hudson and Rod Wales. It was Tim's first experience of living away from home, but a necessary one, as his parents had moved further out of London to the leafy suburb of Virginia Water. The friendly roar of propeller aircraft at Heathrow had given way to the urgent screams of jets, and Len and Joan Dean opted for a quieter life.

Tim, however, wanted to be nearer his friends, and to college. In the summer of 1969 he had abandoned the graphic design course at Ealing, convinced that he should be studying film-making. He was offered a place at the London Film School, although the fees were four times higher than at Ealing because the school was an independent limited company, and not part of the state higher education system. Happily one of his former lecturers wrote a persuasive letter to Tim's local authority, to get the full fees and grant paid. He began a two year course there in January 1970.

The Muswell Hill flat was typical of London's rented and furnished student accommodation. The house was situated in a once affluent residential area, and had seen better days. The carpets were a pale purple colour that no one had imagined could exist in God's rainbow. The people downstairs owned a large cat, Gunther. 'The lads' (as they were nicknamed by their wide circle of friends) called it Gunther Slob because they thought it looked like a fat German psychologist. The cat did not seem to mind; it spent much of its life curled up on their beds.

Lacking the resident care of female domesticity, the bachelor flat quickly took on a shambolic air. Martin Adams, it seems, had been brought up with the wartime dictum which said never throw anything away. He was particularly keen on keeping vegetable stock in pans for weeks at a time, until the others found the stench and sight unbearable. Most of them smoked (hand rolled cigarettes made from one strand of shag tobacco; they were all nearly penniless) and the ashtray was a round film can, placed strategically in the centre of the floor where it was most easily trodden on and tipped over. A stain on the wallpaper marked the spot where a gold-painted avocado pear, aimed by Tony Hudson at Malcolm's head, had ended its brief space flight.

Rod Wales had perfected a nasty leer by contorting his whole face, and he would put it on as a joke when he leaned close to people. He did it in the bathroom one morning as Malcolm was brushing his teeth; Rod then disappeared from view as the rotting floorboard on which he was standing finally gave way. The bathroom was over the hallway, and the hole in the floor had provided a convenient spot from which to see who was coming through the front door.

The circle of friends included women (among them Rod's future wife), who would sometimes set to and tidy the place up. It was not unknown for them to do a whole week's washing up in one session at the sink. Their culinary talents also supplemented the four men's more limited repertoire; Tim was especially clueless and when it was his turn to cook he usually relied on shepherd's pie, or any dish with minced beef as the main ingredient. He did, however, discover breadmaking at this period, but by all accounts he regarded food as no more than a necessary means to an end. His gourmet phase was yet to come.

One of the lady visitors to the flat was Hermione Carline, a niece of Stanley Spencer, the painter. Sometimes Tim and Malcolm would go to Sunday lunch at her parents' home in Hampstead, preceded by drinks on the lawn. The house was full of original paintings by Spencer and Hermione's father, including the working drawing for Spencer's *Resurrection at Cookham* which hangs in the Tate Gallery. It made a pleasant change and sharp contrast to the bachelor flat chaos.

The flat quickly became a social centre and meeting place. If Meryl came across students who needed temporary emergency accommodation she sent them along to 'the lads'; there was always room on the lounge floor. On one occasion an American Christian, dodging the Vietnam War draft on grounds of conscience, came to stay for a week. No one quite knew whence he came nor where he went.

Two regular visitors were to play a particularly important role in Tim's life. Both had been drawn into the circle through the second art students conference, held in November 1969 in the more civilised (although non-residential) surroundings of the Waldegrave Hall near All Souls Church in Langham Place, London. One of them was Norman Stone, who was then studying graphic design in Leeds, not far from his Yorkshire village home. Norman was also interested in film making, and in Tim he found the only person he (and most others) knew who was a Christian, a thinker, and someone who had actually begun training to work in the film industry. They established an immediate rapport; today Norman is an accomplished film director and looks back with gratitude on those discussions with his early mentor.

The other was David Porter. He was studying librarianship in Liverpool and had given a few poetry readings of his own work. He held the others in awe; they seemed to know so much about the arts. They held him in awe, too; poetry was a closed book to many of them at the time. Their mutual admiration soon melted into friendship, however, and David regularly caught the Liverpool to London bus in order to stay with 'the lads' for a weekend. He frequently went to the cinema with the friends, and learnt from Tim how to watch and understand films, looking for the hidden agenda behind the words and images.

Tim himself was also learning. Tony Hudson and Rod Wales were into music, and they enlarged his musical horizons. He discovered the J. Geils rock band, went to one of their concerts and caught one of the few T-shirts thrown into the bopping audience. He developed a lasting appreciation of the fine guitar work of Ry Cooder and the

deep, soulful voice of Joan Armatrading. When the Rolling
Stones came to a free open air concert in Hyde Park, of
course everyone went. The drummer of Screw, a band
which came on before the Stones, was a man called Nick
Brotherwood. He was known to some of the friends and
later joined the Dave Rees Band, which Rod Wales road-
managed and which was one of the early Christian groups
on the secular circuit. Nick became a Christian, joined the
circle of friends, and today is an Anglican clergyman.

Tim and his friends had lived through a brief but major
revolution. The 1960s saw massive changes in the western
way of life; more were to come in the early 1970s, but their
seeds were already sown. Elvis Presley, the Beatles and the
Rolling Stones had changed the entire face of popular
entertainment and brought new values, new questions and
new longings into ordinary homes.

The Macmillan era when 'you'd never had it so good' had
begun to fade, and the CND marchers had failed to halt the
spread of nuclear weapons, and hence the growing threat of
atomic war. Men had walked on the moon, but John F.
Kennedy and Martin Luther King were both assassinated,
and with them the hopes for lasting peace and brotherhood
had begun to die, despite the hippies' belief that the Age of
Aquarius was about to dawn. The pessimism which Hans
Rookmaaker had already perceived in modern art was
slowly creeping into the modern mind. The sociological
retreat into the private house dominated by the con-
versation-killing TV had begun and would not be reversed.
By 1973 the Gulf oil crisis would send western inflation and
unemployment soaring and governments tumbling, and the
fragile economic stability created in post-war Europe
would become a brief fact of history.

In the cultural confusion, the social discontent and the
political decline, Tim and his friends were searching for an
authentic way of expressing the new Christian insights they
were discovering. For most of them that way led, para-
doxically, through an overt rejection, or at least harsh
criticism of, the traditional churches. For some it also led to

excessive behaviour, as the restraints came off and they struggled to find fresh values. Their frequent and loud parties were well oiled with bottles of wine and cans of beer, although by all accounts Tim did not over-indulge to the same degree as some others. He had been drunk only once, and the experience had warned him off repeating it.

He maintained his church links, too, and while living in Muswell Hill sometimes attended Cholmeley Evangelical Church, an open Brethren assembly where he met and made friends with a hospitable couple, Brian and Rachel Griffiths. Brian was then a lecturer at the London School of Economics, a brilliant scholar and teacher who, at the time of writing, has become head of Prime Minister Margaret Thatcher's Policy Studies Unit based at 10 Downing Street.

Like many of Tim's relationships formed during this period, that with the Griffiths became integral to the complex tapestry which enfolded his illnesses. The minor characters in his drama are numerous but each has a significant speaking part at some crucial point in the plot.

And that plot thickens as the scene changes and the characters shift positions, as the bright lights dim and the happy music softens.

The old question was rearing its head again: 'What do you do next?'

The answer was one Tim had not expected.

Five

The French connection

The film industry, they say, is ninety per cent un-employment. Tim had made a couple of 'shorts' at college but they had not impressed potential employers sufficiently. His friend Norman Stone, however, did break into the industry after a post-graduate course at the Royal College of Art. A couple of his student films were shown on British TV and he was soon working regularly with the BBC TV religious department's *Everyman* team.

Tim left the London Film School at the end of 1971. For the next eighteen months he did odd jobs, mostly by returning more permanently to a regular vacation stand-by, working as a decorator and handyman at the Scripture Union London offices. The Muswell Hill flat passed on to other tenants, too, as 'the lads' split up. Tim lived with his sister at Chertsey in Surrey for a time, and Malcolm Doney, also unemployed, went to his parents near Woking in Surrey. Tim and Malcolm occasionally cycled to meet each other halfway between their respective homes, for a drink and a chat. When Malcolm found a job as a packer and messenger in Zwemmer's art bookshop in the Charing Cross Road, he needed a London flat again.

Through Norman Stone, he heard of a couple of rooms going over a junk shop in Highbury Park, north London, and he and Tim moved in. The area, close to Arsenal's soccer stadium, was unpleasant, frequented by drunks who made the walk home from Finsbury Park underground station after the pubs had closed a hazardous affair. The flat was worse, and they soon began to hate it.

The kitchen wall was full of wet rot, so damp that ice formed on it during the cold winter nights. Tim was driven to trying out his handyman skills, repointing and waterproofing it. Once, Malcolm found a mouse in his bed, caught it in a box and threw it out of the window. There was no bath, and the toilet became blocked every few weeks. When the landlord provided a chemical toilet, he inconveniently forgot that there was nowhere to empty it. The toilet and telephone were shared with a family upstairs, a small, wiry and usually drunk Irish labourer and his large and very vocal wife. The couple never spoke to each other; they shouted instead, and usually late into the night. Inevitably, their baby was always crying.

The final straw came after they had been there for some months. Tim was sleeping alone in the flat one night; Malcolm was staying at a rather better place occupied by friends a couple of miles away. It was raining heavily. About midnight there was a huge crash, and something weighty fell on Tim, almost smothering him. He staggered over to the light, and discovered that the ceiling had collapsed. And on the other bed a large chunk of plaster lay where Malcolm's head should have been. Tim dressed, and went to the phone, waking Malcolm and everyone else at the other flat. 'I'm coming round,' he said.

Shaken, he went out into the now quiet streets. There were no taxis to be found, so he trudged all the way in the pouring rain. The next day he wrote once again to the landlord, who was a Christian living on the south coast of England. He had done little to improve the standard of his property so Tim used the only language the landlord seemed to understand: he refused to pay any more rent.

It was perhaps not surprising that in such circumstances – even before the ceiling fell in – Tim was beginning to feel constantly below par. Still not over-concerned about a balanced diet, in the early months of 1973 he was looking more pasty than usual – his skin had always been pale – and he was feeling rather sluggish. It was a slow decline however; he was not fit, but neither did he seem ill.

And good news had come as a tonic, and hope as a spur. There was an unexpected possibility that his days of odd-jobbing were drawing to a close. He had continued to attend the arts students' Bible study. It was now led by Tony Wales (brother of Rod, who had been one of 'the lads'), who had taken over Meryl Fergus' responsibilities at IVF in 1970. He had a more specific brief to visit art colleges nationwide, with a reduced number of technical colleges in the south-east. In April 1973 Tony wrote to him.

Dear Tim,

I'm writing to you in this formal manner in order to invite you to think about the possibility of being my successor as IVF Travelling Secretary to the Art Colleges.

As you know, I've been thinking and praying about this for some time, and this is the fruit of it. We need someone who has the following qualifications:

1. Sound doctrine. 2. An understanding of the contemporary arts. 3. An appreciation of Art College life and mentality. 4. Ability to organise events and people eg. Arts weekends, Professor Rookmaaker's tours, Bible study groups, etc. 5. An ability to meet students (Christian and otherwise) on their own ground with Christian understanding.

All these I believe you possess. Of course there are many things you will want to discuss but in this letter I am simply putting to you the basic proposition. So I'll keep it short.

I suggest that you keep this completely confidential until (a) you've had time to think and pray about it and (b) we've had the opportunity to go over it together. Your parents are, of course, an exception to this.

Let me know as soon as you want to talk it over.

Prayers and love in the Lord,

Tony.

It was not only a potentially new departure for Tim, it also heralded a new development within IVF. He was being offered the opportunity to concentrate exclusively on the art colleges, so quickly had the numbers of Christians grown in them. There was no one else on the circuit who had the right qualifications for the job, although Tim's long, shoulder-length hair and direct, at times abrasive, manner at interviews had some of us in IVF asking Tony rather plaintively, 'Just who is this guy?'

The invitation came as a complete shock to Tim; whatever he had dreamt of doing with his life, it was not this. He had an image of the IVF staff as being a special breed of Christians, far more spiritually advanced than he felt himself to be. He needed little reminding that he was unorthodox in appearance and mildly radical in some of his thinking, at least compared with the stereotype of Oxbridge faith and manners sometimes (but wrongly) assumed to be the IVF badge of office. But then, Tony Wales had long hair, too.

And Tim had begun treading – and had progressed some considerable way along – the intellectual and spiritual path of relating his faith to his work and interests in the film world since that first encounter with Professor Rookmaaker. Nor was he a stranger to Christian theology. He had taken on board the basic truths of Christian doctrine long before his teenage decision to become a disciple of Christ; his conversion had become a matter of reappropriating them in a new context. Around the time of the invitation, he was reading Christian books avidly.

He had even had some experience of giving talks to groups of arts students at conferences, sometimes on quite practical subjects such as how a film is put together. He had occasionally addressed the church youth group and led youth services at Virginia Water when he had lived there briefly with his parents, too. There, he had once displayed his organisational ability by persuading British Rail to stop a late night train at a country station it normally sped through, in order to take youngsters home after a barbecue and gospel concert in the nearby woodlands. But, despite all that, the invitation would still take some serious thought. Tim was not the sort of person to take on something which he did not feel was appropriate, just because other people were sure he could do it; he had to be sure himself.

The idea took root in Tim's mind, but he also had an important engagement to keep with the French film director Robert Bresson. He had become intrigued with Bresson's work while at the London Film School, and had started to write a thesis on it. However he had refused to finish it until he had had an opportunity to talk directly to the film maker.

Bresson's melancholic films were shot in austere scenes with a tight economy of action and dialogue, often dealing with sin, suffering and death. A Roman Catholic, he had been greatly influenced by the Russian novelist Dostoevsky and shared with him a broadly Christian view of man's accountability to God. He looked through the lens at human chaos, asked its cause, and answered the question in the title of one of his films: *The Devil, Probably*. Between the film director and his young admirer there was a meeting of minds, of kindred spirits. Tim saw on the screen a reflection of his own growing perception of the world, and it fascinated him.

Tim travelled to Paris in May 1973, on the Saturday when Second Division soccer club Sunderland beat the mighty Leeds United in the English Cup Final. It was a bad start; he would have preferred to be at home watching the game on TV. Worst of all, he was alone, broke, and tongue-tied, in a foreign city.

French had been one of his worst subjects at school. During his two years at Isleworth Grammar School, the French teacher – who was a Greek – took an instant dislike to him. The feeling was mutual. Indeed, the whole class was terrified of the man who would make pupils do handstands against the door, often for long periods, as a punishment for minor offences. Tim's workbook disappeared after he had handed it in to the teacher for marking; it reappeared a month later only after he had been made to pay for a new one – and there was no refund. This experience had prejudiced him against the French language and eroded his confidence in his ability to speak it, despite a more humane teacher at Woodfield Secondary School. Fortunately, Bresson's films were subtitled for English audiences, and the director himself was bi-lingual.

Tim had several days to kill before the interview was scheduled, so he began to explore the French capital. He had the address of British Protestant Christians working as missionaries in the mainly Catholic city. They gave him a bed for a couple of nights, but the long-haired and rather unkempt young man clad in jeans was clearly out of place, and he moved into a student hostel for the rest of the week.

He scoured the streets looking for cafes where he could buy a meal for less than a pound, and discovered a seedy Algerian place where his rudimentary knowledge of French just enabled him to identify chicken and chips on the menu. He observed French police patrolling the poorer areas of the city in groups of five, armed with sub-machine guns. He sniffed the distinctive and irritating odour of the Metro underground, unrelated, it seemed, to any other smell known to mankind. He walked along the banks of the Seine, and found them far less romantic than the legends portray.

And he toured the art galleries. In the Louvre he discovered its 400,000 masterpieces of centuries competing for wall space, hung so closely together under reflecting glass that it was almost impossible to see them. He got the briefest glimpse of Leonardo's *Mona Lisa*. As if they were characters in a living cartoon, sightseers jostled around the world's most famous portrait, staring up at it through cardboard periscopes. Mona Lisa, reputed to have been the wife of a rich Florentine merchant, stared back with her enigmatic smile which contained more than a touch of irony, perhaps even cynicism.

At the student hostel Tim met another Englishman, who happened to be a Roman Catholic. He had someone to talk to at last; Paris became a little less lonely. The weather was pleasant, and one day they wandered down the Boulevard Saint-Michel lined with bookshops, past the Sorbonne and the student hub of the city, pausing at pavement cafes to drink and talk. In the evening they crossed the Seine by the Pont Saint-Michel, and sat together in a dark alcove in a dim red-lit American basement cafe. Above the noise of the music, they were discussing Christianity; the English Catholic was asking the questions, and Tim was offering him answers. The young man was troubled by the problem of suffering.

'Why, if he is loving, does God allow evil?' he asked.

'You can't blame God for evil,' Tim replied. 'The concept of the fall of man means that humanity in general bears the responsibility for evil in the world. God is the sovereign ruler over all things. He's just, he's righteous, he's loving. Whatever is going on can't be handled better than by God.'

The encounter was an important confidence-booster for Tim. It showed him that Tony Wales' evaluation of his character had some basis in fact; he could indeed relate easily to complete strangers and talk meaningfully to them about his Christian faith – a vital part of the proposed IVF job. He could look back on the apparently pointless past eighteen months and see them as a necessary time for growing and maturing.

In retrospect Tim reckoned the encounter had a touch of divine irony, even comedy, about it. After all, a God who could conceive of the comic penguin and create the brightly coloured parakeet cannot entirely be without a sense of humour. And the key to humour is timing.

It was almost as if God in his heaven smiled knowingly at his young follower's confident explanation of the universe's secrets, and without a trace of malice or vindictiveness, said, 'OK, my son, that's what you believe; now you must go and put it into practice. You've talked theoretically about suffering; now you will find out what it's like in practice, and whether what you believe is true.'

Three weeks later Tim was admitted to hospital with cancer.

Six

Scattered pieces of jigsaw

When Tim had received Tony Wales' letter asking him to consider taking over as IVF arts students travelling secretary, he was working again at Scripture Union. It was taking him an unusually long time to paint a corridor on the top floor of the Marylebone Lane offices; he was tiring quickly. Life was becoming little more than working and sleeping; he often went to bed early, soon after his evening meal.

He was also having regular sharp headaches and fleeting visual blackouts. He had had brief blackouts, perhaps twice a year, while at secondary school. They usually preceded a migraine; the outside ring of his vision became blurred, and the blur slowly closed in, as if he were looking through a lens around which someone was smearing Vaseline. Now, however, they were occurring several times a week, and were quite different. His vision resembled an old TV set being turned off and on, the picture narrowing to a dot in the centre of the screen for maybe twenty seconds, then growing back to full size again. But he had no sense of being ill or even dizzy.

He decided that it was time to visit the doctor for a check-up and went to his local surgery when he returned to London from Paris. He was not seen by the doctor he was registered with, but by another in the group practice. The doctor listened as Tim described his symptoms, and prescribed painkillers.

As he got up to leave, Tim added, 'By the way, I've had a stiff neck for ages. Could you look at it?' It was a casual after-thought; he had twisted his neck while dancing at a party some months before, and he found moving it slightly difficult.

The doctor parted Tim's shoulder-length hair, and pulled his long bushy beard away from his neck. On the left side of his neck was a huge swelling. It was as large as a grapefruit. Tim never wore a tie, and so never buttoned his collar (which would now have been impossible). His hair and beard covered his neck and concealed the swelling. He had never noticed it. It had grown slowly over a period of time. Saying little, the doctor sat him down again and gave him a thorough check-up. He found traces of eczema on his legs.

'I want you to go and see a consultant at the Whittington Hospital,' he said. He already suspected that Tim had a form of cancer, but naturally said nothing at the time.

Tim knew where the Whittington was; it was his area hospital in north London. The place looked shabby and uninviting, conjuring up the image of a nineteenth-century workhouse for the poor. Besides, London is a sprawling place and public transport did not directly connect Tim's Highbury Park flat with the hospital, and he had no car.

'Couldn't I go to the Middlesex Hospital instead?' he asked. 'I'm working very close to it and it would be much easier to get to.'

The doctor had every reason to agree. He happened to know that the Middlesex staff were well experienced in treating the disease Tim had probably contracted. He addressed the referral letter there.

It was as if scattered pieces of some cosmic jigsaw were beginning to join up and form a pattern. Tim himself had never heard of the Middlesex Hospital until he had literally come across it by accident earlier in the year.

One week he had joined a crew from the London Film School to shoot a film for the Hong Kong Government; the dialogue was entirely in Cantonese. On location at a student centre near Notting Hill Gate, the crew used heavy two-kilowatt lights fitted with 'barn doors', metal flaps

which helped direct the beam. As Tim picked up a light to
load it into the crew's van, a barn door which had been
wrongly mounted on it slid out and crushed his big toe.

He lay in the back of the van in agony. The crew were
driving along Oxford Street in central London late at night
and decided to take him to the nearest hospital – which
happened to be the Middlesex. The duty casualty officer
saw that bleeding beneath the nail was causing the pain; he
burned a small hole in the nail, releasing the blood and
relieving the pain. 'If I'd never had that experience I'd
never have asked to go to the Middlesex.'

And if he had never asked . . .? Questions of that order
cannot be answered, at least not in this life; no computer
could work out the limitless consequences of even one
different action or reaction, because of the infinite number
of new human choices it would bring into play. Life is much
more than a mechanical chain-reaction. Yet the fact that
Tim did ask was to prove crucial for his eventual recovery.
Research on his condition was in its infancy, and the staff at
the Middlesex were closely in touch with the latest develop-
ments in treatment. Any long delay in his eventual referral
to its specialist staff would almost certainly have been fatal.
As it turned out, he was to be treated only in the nick of
time.

But he was given no hint of urgency when he made his
way to the hospital on Monday 21 May 1973. Close to
London's famous Oxford Street shopping area and the
BBC's tall grey Broadcasting House in Regent Street, the
present Middlesex Hospital was built in the late 1920s and
early 1930s, incorporating elements of the elegant
grandeur of the Edwardian era. Two seven-floor wings
front onto Mortimer Street, a fancy cornice separating the
first two stone-faced floors from the brick-faced floors
above. Joining the wings, and set back from the road, is a
crosspiece with a temple-like archway sculpted into its
centre and rising from ground to roof. The small courtyard
in front of the entrance and between the wings might once
have lent the place a quiet, dignified air, but now it is

cluttered with staff cars.

The surrounding area is riddled with narrow streets lined with mostly functional, plain buildings from five to eight floors high. Many of them have been taken over by clothing wholesalers, their upper floors let as offices or apartments. There is little space close at hand where visitors can park cars; the hustle and bustle which has always been part of London life is nowhere more obvious than around the Middlesex Hospital.

Tim was due to see Professor Semple at the Outpatients Department. The Professor examined Tim's neck and asked him to come back to the hospital as an in-patient for a few days. He said he wanted to do a biopsy (take a small piece of tissue from the lump) under general anaesthetic.

Tim had little knowledge of hospital procedures; he had no idea that a doctor's request for an immediate operation spelt urgency, because of the normally long waiting lists for minor surgery. To his mind, he had a more important engagement; he had planned to spend the following week-end with his old friend Norman Stone in Yorkshire. He asked if the operation could be postponed for a week.

Professor Semple agreed; it was to be the first of Tim's many experiences of the staff's relaxed approach. They were firm when they needed to be, but they believed that a patient's emotional well-being can play an important part in his response to physical illness, especially cancer. Tim was not to be thrust into an inflexible regime in which conformity ruled with an iron fist.

Norman Stone lived with his parents at Thornhill Edge, a small village on the northern borders of the rugged Peak District. Although only a few miles south of the urban sprawl of Leeds, Bradford and Huddersfield, it was quiet and unspoiled. The house where the Stone family lived overlooked a steep-sided valley. From the rough wall on the opposite side of the road to the house Tim looked down on a hawk hovering on the rising air currents; far below a trout stream bubbled across the valley floor.

It was a place where freedom and fun almost hung, like

the hawk, in the air; a place for rambles across the hills with
Norman and Bracken, the Stones' red setter. The dog was a
constant source of amusement. He had been taught a series
of codewords so that he could apparently do complicated
maths; asked the square root of sixty-four he would
obediently bark eight times. So obedient was Bracken that
he would sit with a biscuit on his paws and refuse to eat it
until he was told to. It proved a rather unfortunate trick
when friends who were looking after him one day forgot the
codeword and had to leave the dog drooling over his biscuit
for several hours!

Norman's father was the first minister of the village
Baptist Church since the previous century. When he had
visited the church with a view to becoming its pastor, there
were six people in the congregation. But he felt strongly
that it was where God wanted him. As the six faithfuls were
unlikely to be able to support a family man, he took a job as
a sales rep, visiting Yorkshire shops professionally in the
daytime and visiting the villagers pastorally in the evenings.
His faith had been justified. The congregation had grown
rapidly and was soon able to support him full-time.

Tim had been there several times, and he had got to
know some of the youth group, always chuckling over the
surnames of the two Jills – Hill (who was tall) and Mountain
(who was short). So it was quite natural for Norman's
father to ask him to speak to the young people after the
Sunday evening service. Norman interviewed him, and
Tim spoke informally about his belief in God's kingship, or
sovereignty, over a person's life, and especially over the
future.

He instanced his own experience. He had spent a year
and a half doing odd jobs, he said, without knowing how he
could make a move into doing something more purposeful.
He believed that God had some purpose in store for him,
but he had so far been unable to identify it. (Protocol did
not allow him to mention the current IVF possibility.) It
had not been an easy time, he admitted, but none the less
he told them, 'I do believe God has been in control of the

past months.'

But before the future became plainer, he had a more immediate challenge to face. 'I have to go into hospital next week,' he continued. 'Of this I'm sure; God wants me to be there. So I'll be content to be there, even though I don't know why. Even if I have cancer, I know that I'm in God's hands.'

It was one of those off-the-cuff remarks which is spoken before it is even thought through. He no more believed that he could have cancer than that he was Chinese. Not being a person who was over-concerned about health matters, it never entered his head that there could be anything seriously wrong with him. He did not even know that lumps could be caused by cancer.

'I was overstating the case; I am prone to exaggeration at times. I was just so convinced that I was in God's hands, even though I'd had a rough time being unemployed or under-employed.'

Tim spent the evening before he went into hospital with friends. As usual in such gatherings, they were drinking moderate quantities of alcohol. The branch of the Christian Church in which Tim had been reared usually branded alcohol as at best a danger to be avoided, at worst an outright evil, a tradition of which his father had once fallen foul. To Tim and his friends, that was tantamount to adding to the ten commandments, especially when one of the psalms sang the praises of a creator God who provided 'wine that gladdens the heart of man', and one of the gospels stated that the first miracle Jesus performed was to turn 150 gallons of water into top quality wine at a wedding celebration (Ps. 104:15; John 2:1–10).

But that did not make him insensitive to the scruples of his fellow-Christians. At Thornhill Edge, the deep-rooted Yorkshire tradition was that a man went to the chapel or the pub, but never both. To have opened a bottle of wine at the Stones' home or to have taken Norman down to 'the local' would have been grossly insensitive, however artificial he himself regarded the division. No less a person

than St Paul, after all, had recognised that his own lack of
conscience about eating meat which had been butchered
with an accompanying pagan ritual did not give him licence
to offend the consciences of Christians who considered
eating such food to be unethical. 'Be careful,' he wrote,
'that the exercise of your freedom does not become a
stumbling block to the weak' (1 Cor. 8:9).

On the night before his admission there were no such
problems to contend with. A new one, however, made an
appearance. Tim experienced some physical pains after
drinking beer. To those who knew about such things, it was
a small but telling sign that the disease they suspected he
had was in an advanced stage.

The next morning, Thursday 31 May, he presented himself at Sandhurst Ward, a general medical ward on the first
floor of the Middlesex Hospital's east wing.

Professor Semple had told him he would probably be in
hospital 'for a few days'. He was to be there for over two
months, with only a brief break at home in the middle. The
biopsy confirmed the doctors' fears – and it was not to be
the only surgical operation Tim needed.

Seven

The truth at last

Recovering from the effects of the anaesthetic, Tim began looking round Sandhurst Ward. It was a strange new world. His boyhood hatred of hospitals had gone; in its place was a growing curiosity. He began making up his own amusements, his fertile mind delighting in new things to discover. He worked out the ranking of the nurses simply by watching, listening, and observing their different coloured belts, caps and dresses. There were things to do in the ward, like making tea (he was not confined to bed for long after the biopsy), and there were men in it from all walks of life to meet and listen to.

The ward was high ceilinged, with green tiles on the walls, and a separate television lounge. A few of the beds were on an enclosed balcony overlooking a quadrangle in the centre of the hospital which, complete with a neat shrubbery and a working fountain, might almost have been lifted out of a Cambridge college.

For the first couple of weeks, nothing much was done to Tim apart from regular blood tests. But something was happening to him. He began to get feverish night sweats, when he would awaken out of a deep sleep and feel as if he were bathing in a river. He was soaked, and his pyjamas and the bed clothes had to be changed. His temperature was down below normal during the daytime, and he was losing weight. Despite leading a sedentary life, he was asleep for longer and longer periods, sometimes sleeping or dozing for up to fifteen hours a day. To give him more privacy and quiet, he was moved from the main open ward into a single-bed room just off it.

When he had first entered hospital, he was reading heavyweight books avidly. He had recently read some of Arthur Koestler's novels, and had become fascinated by them. Having heard that a new Koestler book had just been published, he asked if the hospital library could get it for him. It was not long before *The Roots of Coincidence* was on his bedside locker, and he was discovering Koestler's debunking of certain modern physics theories and defence of the possibilities of extra-sensory perception. But Tim's concentration began to fail; his mind found it increasingly hard to focus on the arguments of such books. Within a week or so his reading matter was largely restricted to the cartoon escapades of *Asterix the Gaul* by the Frenchmen Goscinny and Udezo. The superbly-drawn graphics and witty story lines created the mental diversion he needed. (One heroic character in an Asterix story is rather aptly named Timandahalf!) He even found that he could not concentrate on the Bible for very long.

Also beside his bed were books on the films of French director Jean Luc Godard. Tim was due to give a talk on Godard's work at an art students' conference early in July, and to show his film *Alphaville*, an avant garde criticism of growing social institutionalism. One morning the books were on top of the pile as the pharmacist came on his daily ward round to check on patients' reactions to their drugs, but Tim was not in his room at the time. The pharmacist, David, was also interested in Godard's films, and made a mental note to call back and meet the owner of the books. He did so, and the two men struck up a genial relationship; when Tim was fit they occasionally went to the cinema together. A year later that relationship would prove important in helping Tim through a traumatic period of treatment.

David was not the only member of the medical staff with whom Tim talked, however. He still neither worried nor feared; he did not know he had anything to worry about or to fear. So he began to quiz them about what they were doing, and why; he was curious about the workings of the body he had lived with for twenty-three years but had never taken much notice of before. The 'them and us' division of staff and patients started to break down. Medical students began using Tim's side room as a regular port of call for coffee and a chat; the nurses would come in to talk, too, especially when he had the night-sweats.

It was a two-way affair; relationships were being established by the staff as well; it was not simply a matter of Tim's interest in his new environment. When Dr Jelliffe, his Consultant, first examined him, he came into the ward without his white coat 'uniform', and spent some time finding out who Tim was, what he did and what he liked. Only then did he add, 'I suppose I ought to examine you'. Tim's response was to discover the medical equivalent of *Who's Who* in the doctors' office, and look up Professor Semple and Dr Jelliffe, to learn more about the consultants in charge of his case.

The atmosphere was sufficiently relaxed to allow him out of the hospital occasionally. He would go for a walk or a meal with friends, or visit a bookshop. On Sundays he could stroll along Mortimer Street to attend a church service at All Souls Langham Place, next door to the BBC. Tired he might be, but he was not immobile, nor physically helpless enough to be confined within the hospital for twenty-four hours a day.

Many of his waking hours were spent watching television. It occupied his mind without draining it. He discovered for the first time that he could enjoy watching the native British game of cricket. He followed the whole of a five-day test match between England and New Zealand. And, true to character, once the fascination of the game took hold of him, he became interested in its details, including the way the state of the wicket (the playing area) affected the pace, bounce and turn of the ball. There were the Wimbledon tennis championships to watch, too, a whole fortnight of top class sport, during which he could assess the varying form of the stars.

During the evenings, however, he faced a problem. The majority of men in the ward who were able to walk to the TV lounge wanted to watch the commercial channel with its preponderance of soap operas and dramas. Tim wanted to see some of the programmes on BBC 1 and 2. Eventually he found that there was a TV set in the medical students' teaching room at one end of the ward. Nothing ventured, nothing gained; he asked if he could use it – no lectures or discussions were held there in the evenings. The staff raised no objection and he had it to himself until a woman in a neighbouring ward, who had similar TV preferences, was let in on the secret and came to join him. The nurses sometimes even brought his evening drink to his personal TV room.

On Wednesday 13 June Tim celebrated his twenty-third birthday. He did not tell the staff until midday, but by late afternoon they had given him greetings cards. And then his friends turned up.

All hospitals are the same; the printed notices are standard. 'No more than two visitors are allowed at the bedside at any one time.' Thirteen people turned up that evening to see Tim; being in a side-ward the spontaneous party was not overly disruptive for the other patients. Two lady friends each brought him chocolate birthday cakes they had made. Tony Dean came in laden with wine and beer which the visitors appreciated more than his brother for whom alcohol still gave pain.

There was laughter and gaiety. Even though Tim's world had come to a virtual standstill for the two weeks he had so far been in hospital, the world outside was still spinning; friends and relatives continued to live, work, talk and play, to achieve ambitions and make mistakes. There were things to hear, things to tell, things to discuss. In America President Nixon had denied all knowledge of the Watergate scandal. The cold war had defrosted a little with the signing of a USA-USSR arms limitation agreement. The cod war had got rougher, however, with British frigates defending trawlers within the disputed Icelandic fishing limits.

And as everyone knew almost everyone else, the unfamiliar pale green walls, the distinct shortage of chairs and the cold uncarpeted floor were minor distractions. Not for the last time, Tim's hospital bed became a new central London meeting place for his circle of acquaintances.

It was a happy interlude, but was followed by some less pleasant medical tests. There was a kidney test, an intravenous pyelogram, which was an unpleasant injection into his groin followed by an X-ray. He also had a brain scan to see if there was any obvious cause for his blackouts. It proved no more than that he had a brain! The blackouts were probably caused by the pressure exerted on his blood vessels by the massive lump on his neck.

One of the tests turned him a delicate shade of green. The day after his birthday, green dye was injected between his toes in order to distinguish his lymph vessels (part of the body's defensive system) from his veins. Then the doctors attached a Heath-Robinson contraption to his feet, looking rather like an overgrown test tube rack from a school chemistry laboratory. They gave him a local anaesthetic then cut his feet open, inserting needles into his lymph vessels. The needles were linked by tubes to containers on the rack which were filled with a golden-yellow, translucent fluid. A heavy metal bar forced plungers into the containers, slowly pushing the fluid into his feet for three hours. The fluid was a radio-sensitive tracer, and Tim was wheeled downstairs for an X-ray of his entire lymphatic system, known as a lymphangiogram. The green dye worked through his body and persisted for some days, giving him a Martian-like appearance. This rather cumbersome procedure, like the kidney test, is now sometimes replaced by the sophisticated EMI body scanner, which had not been developed in 1973.

One morning, a medical student was taking blood from Tim in a routine test. They were talking. Ever observant, Tim saw the name 'Hodgkins' on the paperwork.

'What's Hodgkins mean?' he asked.

The student was nonplussed for a moment, then replied, 'Oh, it's probably the department the sample is sent to.'

It was not, and the student knew it. Tim had seen the name of his disease, but it was not the student's duty to reveal the fact. He hated having to lie; he and other medical students knew that Tim was capable of accepting the truth and of coming to terms with it. They raised the matter with Professor Semple, and urged him to break the silence. After some discussion, he decided to do so. One evening, about seven o'clock, he came into the ward. Tim was out of bed, sitting on the desk in the centre of the main ward, talking to the nurses.

'Can I have a word with you, Tim?' he asked.

They went into the side room where Tim had his bed. The Registrar, the house doctor, the ward sister and staff nurse all followed. Tim sat in the armchair, the professor perched on the bed, the others stood together between door and bed.

'You've got something called Hodgkin's Disease,' began Professor Semple.

A lump came into Tim's throat. Maybe it was the way he said 'Hodgkin's Disease'. The word cancer was not used; it was superfluous.

'Had you had it a couple of years ago we probably wouldn't have been able to do anything for you,' he continued. The lump grew larger. 'We can't guarantee to cure you, but we're hopeful that we can get you back to living a reasonably normal life.'

It was far more serious than Tim had imagined. He needed to get out, to walk, to think. 'Can I go out for a short walk?' he asked.

Unusually the request was rejected. Dr Jelliffe needed to see him soon. Tim compromised. He paced the long corridors of the Middlesex Hospital, trying to come to terms with the news. He had to share it. His parents were on holiday in Canada; they had known of his need for a biopsy but no one in the family had realised it was serious enough for them to cancel their plans. He returned to Sandhurst

Ward and used the pay-phone trolley from his room. He called his brother Tony; he was out, but Cynthia, his wife, answered. Tim told her what had happened.

As soon as she had put the phone down Cynthia went to a neighbour, who was a doctor, and asked him what it meant. He told her in simple terms what Hodgkin's Disease was; Tim had cancer.

Hodgkin's Disease was named after Thomas Hodgkin, a London doctor who first described it in 1832. It affects the lymphatic system, the body's main defence against infection. The system is a network of lymph vessels (like veins) throughout the body linking the lymph nodes (often wrongly called 'glands') which often and quite naturally become enlarged when the body is fighting an infection. The disease begins when cells in one node multiply in an uncontrolled manner, but what triggers it is at present unknown.

It is a rare disease, affecting about one in every 25,000 people, mostly men between twenty and forty years of age. It can develop in four stages. In stage one, the patient has infected lymph nodes in one place (the neck being the most common). In the second stage, nodes are infected in two localities on the same side of the diaphragm (that is, either above or below it). By stage three, the patient has infected nodes in two or more places on both sides of the diaphragm. In stage three-B the disease becomes 'advanced', with the patient developing symptoms such as night-sweats, fevers, loss of weight, pain after drinking alcohol, and extreme drowsiness. In stage four, the disease has spread to vital organs such as the liver.

Today, the cure rate for patients in the early stages is high – eighty per cent survive for five or more years without a trace of the disease (which is the usual medical definition of a cure). At least forty per cent of people with Advanced Hodgkin's are cured. But in 1973 the success rate was much lower and the treatment more crude.

And Tim was known to be in stage three-B. Whether the disease had spread to the fourth and final stage would not be known until he paid another visit to the operating theatre.

Eight

Breaking the pain barrier

'I think I picked myself up pretty quickly after they broke the news. I still did not feel I was at death's door. I knew I had time to think about it and come to terms with it. They hoped I would get back to a reasonable life. They gave me no indication of any time scale. I'm not sure I ever asked. There was a sense in which I learned to live from day to day.'

Once he had recovered from the initial shock, Tim's old single-mindedness and curiosity fused into a powerful determination. 'I said to myself: I've got this illness and it's going to screw my life up for a while. So I'm going to find out everything I can about it.'

So when Dr Jelliffe came in and said he wanted to take out Tim's spleen, his patient replied that he did not know he even had one; but as he obviously had, what was it? A fist-sized organ in the upper left abdomen, he was told. Thought in medieval times to be the seat of anger and melancholy, it regulates the quantity and quality of blood flowing through the body. Tim could afford to lose it without facing the prospect of his blood supply drying up, because the liver and bone marrow exercise the same function and can compensate for the loss of the spleen. The operation would also include a biopsy on his liver, Dr Jelliffe said; a small piece would be removed for laboratory examination.

Once again, Tim asked for a concession before going under the surgeon's knife. Before, it had been a weekend in Yorkshire with Norman Stone. This time it was a wedding in Oxfordshire on 23 June 1973; the groom was David Porter the poet, who was by then lecturing in music bibliography at Liverpool Polytechnic. His bride was Tricia Widdison, a photographer who specialised in unposed pictures of people living and working in their natural surroundings.

It was an unconventional event, recapturing some of the charm which conveyor-belt weddings conducted according to custom can squeeze out. It was held on the tennis court of a large shooting lodge, borrowed from friends for the occasion. A children's orchestra followed Tricia onto the court and played to the guests on the lawn after the open-air ceremony conducted by Dick Keyes and Ranald Mac-Auley of the L'Abri Fellowship in Hampshire.

Tim travelled by car north-west from London to the Oxfordshire countryside with Meryl Fergus and Malcolm Doney, not noticing anything unusual in the fact that his two friends were together; he was used to them being at the same events with the same crowd of people. His time in hospital caused him to miss the budding romance. Still long-haired and bearded, he wore white trousers and a double-breasted pin-stripe jacket, which he had been given second-hand. He still had his hospital identity tag on his wrist – it could only be cut off when he was eventually discharged – a fact which caused some amusement among his friends.

It was a tiring day for him, but a refreshing one as well. He received an emotional boost from a relatively normal day out in the world with his friends, and it was a particularly happy occasion at that. It gave him new personal strength to face the operation and whatever lay beyond it.

Although he was able to attend the wedding, Tim knew he would miss the arts students' conference in the first week of July. Held at a country house in Essex bought by pop singer Cliff Richard as a place where artists and media people could explore Christianity, it drew together, among the speakers and seminar leaders, a number of Tim's friends. Some, like him, were beginning to make their

mark as experts rather than students; others were a little
longer in the tooth.

Chief among them was Graham Birtwistle, who had
taught art history at Leicester Polytechnic but who was by
then teaching in Professor Rookmaaker's department in
Amsterdam, and who had become a personal friend to
Tim. Nigel Goodwin was there, a former actor and the
first director of the Arts Centre Group, where the London
Bible study group met. So was Gordon Gray, the Director
of Scripture Union's Modern Communications Unit (later
renamed the Sound and Vision Unit); Philip Miles, a
graphic designer at the Victoria and Albert Museum, who
twelve years later would work with Tim on another
Pioneering project at an equally uncertain point in his
medical history; Patrick Wood, son of the then Bishop of
Norwich and a member of the Ballet Rambert Company;
David Porter, too, with his new bride Tricia mounting an
exhibition of her pictures; and even Tim's future
biographer and departmental boss at IVF, giving the Bible
readings on the Christian view of man.

Although he was not among the official list of speakers,
Norman Stone was due to share in Tim's seminar on the
relation of film to TV. While that could be done without
Tim, it seemed more than unfortunate to Norman that
Tim's analysis of Godard's *Alphaville* would also be
missing when the film was shown at the conference. Always
the ideas man, Norman realised that it could be done – on
video. Only hours before Tim was due to have his spleen
removed, Norman, who was then a student at the Royal
College of Art post-graduate Film and Television School,
struggled into the hospital with borrowed college equip-
ment – lightweight video recorders had yet to be invented.
Tim gave his introduction for *Alphaville* facing the camera
in his dressing gown.

To those of us who watched the large black and white TV
screen a few days later, he seemed the same lively Tim we
had always known. In fact, he had changed dramatically
within twenty-four hours of the video being shot.

The wedding behind him, the video in the can, Tim went into the operating theatre on Friday 29 June. That night he moaned and sometimes screamed in his troubled sleep. He awoke the following day in intense pain. 'I had the experience of feeling more pain than I can possibly imagine existed. The painkillers weren't strong enough to contain it. It was excruciating.'

The pain blotted everything else out of his mind. His horizons had shrunk to encompass only the post-operative agonies which racked him from head to foot. His memories of the past and his awareness of art, politics, even his faith, family and friends – all were temporarily veiled from his consciousness. 'It seemed as if my whole life had been one of pain. I could see no end to the pain, either. It seemed that everything I had ever known was pain, and that everything I would know was pain.'

Standing at the foot of his bed as he emerged from the blank world of anaesthetised unconsciousness into the nightmare of reality was Alison, an Australian nurse he had got to know a little during the days before the operation. Contrary to custom, the doctors had sent him back after the surgery to Sandhurst Ward where there were people he knew, rather than to a surgical ward. The familiar friendly face as he struggled with the fearsome agony was extremely reassuring.

He was back in the main open ward, in a bed directly opposite the nurses' desk so that he was under constant observation. Totally drained of energy, it took him all the effort he could muster to try to stop groaning. He repeatedly failed. He apologised to the man in the next bed, who told him in no uncertain terms not to worry about it.

The man owned a pub, and was in hospital with jaundice. He provided one of the many interludes of light relief which punctuated hospital life. He had been quizzed at great length by a psychiatrist who was trying to get to the causes of the 'problems' which were supposedly leading him to drink a lot. Somehow the specialist had failed to notice his patient's occupation, much to the publican's amusement.

There was indeed a high level of humour on the wards, slightly warped in the circumstances but born of the human companionship, fellowship almost, which frequently arises when people suffer together at close quarters. There was a man with chronic diarrhoea who made light of his frequent and long visits to the lavatory by inventing epithets such as 'diarrhoea is the thief of time'. One patient had suffered a severe stroke; no humour there but plenty of support: the others taught him to write and talk again.

So, when a fellow-patient was brought back from the operating theatre moaning with pain, there were no angry looks or muttered complaints from the men he had left a few hours earlier. It was part of the unspoken deal; they would be laughing together again soon.

That was Saturday; with Sunday would come Tim's first visitors since the operation. He was determined to be out of bed when they arrived. Still dressed in a pale linen hospital gown, he got into the bedside armchair, helped by the nurses. They had put an inflated tyre inner-tube on it, covered with a sheepskin, to make it more comfortable.

He was still very weak and in considerable pain. He felt haggard; he did not realise quite how bad he looked.

All the visitors that day and over the following week went away with a deep sense of shock. 'I understand that I looked like something out of the Belsen wartime concentration camp.' Tim had lost forty pounds of weight; he was down to eight stone (112 pounds). His cheeks were hollow and deathly white; his arms were just skin and bone. The massive lump on his neck, however, was as big as ever. A drip fed strength-giving fluid into his right arm (because he is left handed), but his head kept sinking to his chest. His normally lucid tongue found conversation almost impossible.

Rod Wales came with his wife Alison. Tim's bed was clearly visible from the double doors leading into the ward, and when Alison caught her first glimpse of him she turned straight back; the sight made her feel ill.

Graham Birtwistle came to London from the arts

students' conference in Essex; he was profoundly shaken by the contrast between Tim on the video and Tim as he had become.

When his parents and sister Verity, with her husband Mervyn, arrived that Sunday afternoon, after his friends had left, Tim had had enough. He was very tired; he felt miserable beyond words. He greeted his family and then burst into tears. He had been in hospital for a month, and had been crushed by a major operation. He knew he was seriously ill, and did not know what the future held – if indeed he had any future. 'I had used up and gone beyond the very deepest reserve of my emotional resources.'

The family held back their own grief until they drove home, when Verity and her mother wept in the back seat of the car for much of the journey. Len and Joan Dean went to a service at their church that evening; when Tim was being prayed for with great concern, Len broke down too. Suddenly, it was plain to everyone how serious the situation really was.

On Wednesday Tim was moved into a bed on the balcony, where the sun shone in through the long windows and where he could look down on the pleasant quadrangle below. A West Indian cleaner saw him one morning later in the week, and began crying. He had looked ghastly after the operation, and when she saw the empty bed he had vacated in the main ward, she assumed he had died. Her tears were those of relief, and gave Tim a fresh insight into the strong human concern which even strangers can feel for one another. 'I was completely taken aback by this, it staggered me. Who was I to her?'

Slowly, the pain subsided. It was a crude matter of trial and error to discover the effective combinations of pain-killers. And as he reflected on the experience, Tim realised that there are two good things about pain.

One is that it is a warning signal that something is wrong. What can make cancer so insidious is that it may not be accompanied by pain until it has reached an advanced (and therefore more difficult to treat) stage. Pain can be a problem, but so can its absence. If he had felt pain in the months before his visit to the doctor, he would have sought advice earlier, but the gradual weakening he experienced went unnoticed – like his short-sightedness as a young child – until it reached a point when it began to disable him.

The other good thing is that the human mind cannot remember pain. 'I cannot recall the pain. I can remember having the experience of intense pain, but not the pain itself. I thank God I can't; otherwise life would be unbearable. I can recall it now only as an abstract concept.' Perhaps that is one reason why people are encouraged too readily to 'grin and bear it'; their advisors have forgotten what their own pains were like.

What Tim did remember for years to come was his first solid meal a couple of days after the operation. Never had scrambled egg on toast tasted so good. It seemed the greatest meal he had ever had; it was like nectar to his starved palate. Malcolm Doney added to his ecstasy by bringing him two cans of Heinz Cream of Tomato Soup. So eager was he for food that he later had to apologise to the nurses for being impatient.

His recovery was remarkably quick. When Professor Semple came to him with the histology reports, there was some good news mingled with the bad. His spleen had been cancerous and enlarged beyond repair, and had had to be removed. But his liver was clean. He had not reached stage four of Advanced Hodgkin's Disease. Professor Semple read him the reports verbatim. Tim's curiosity and ability to cope had returned; he stopped the reader each time he used an unfamiliar word, and asked for and received an explanation of it.

Ten days after the operation he was fit enough to go to his parents' home in Virginia Water. It was Monday 9 July; he had a month to recuperate before the start of a course of intensive drug treatment to attempt to kill the cancer. Or so everyone thought.

Nine

Restored to life

Exactly a fortnight after leaving the Middlesex Hospital to recuperate at his parents' home in Virginia Water, Surrey, Tim was experiencing more abdominal pain. On Monday 23 July he went to the doctor's surgery just across the road. He was attended by a doctor who had done some of his training at the Middlesex and had worked with Dr Jelliffe's department. He examined Tim and did not see any reason to send him back there prematurely.

As he left the surgery, Tim met a woman who had led the young people's group at the parish church, which Tim had occasionally attended a few years earlier. They stopped to talk briefly; he could not stand for long. In her eyes, he looked terrible – so terrible, in fact, that she was convinced he was close to death. When she got home she called her friends and asked them to attend a special meeting at her house the following Thursday evening, to pray specifically for Tim. She did not tell him at the time.

The following morning the pain was worse. Tim made the uncomfortable short walk to the surgery again. This time the doctor decided he should be admitted to hospital at once. However, it was twenty miles away. Public transport was out of the question; and an ambulance would take an emergency case only to the nearest local hospital, unless it was booked well in advance.

Tim's mother had a car but she was terrified of driving in London's dense but fast-moving traffic. So she took him to Heathrow Airport, where his father still worked, and Len Dean drove his ailing son into central London. Tim could by now barely walk because of the pain. He went into the casualty unit and was taken from there to Greenhow Ward, in the hospital's Barnato-Joel wing. It was one of the cancer wards, and at the time was painted a dingy, depressing green. It did not, like Sandhurst, look out over the calm oasis of the quadrangle, but onto the narrow, congested side streets. Tim was given drugs to control the pain, although they did not remove it altogether.

On Wednesday Dr Jelliffe ordered a bone marrow test to be taken. It was not a pleasant experience. Tim was given a local anaesthetic and then a syringe was screwed into his chest to draw off the bone marrow fluid. As usual in such circumstances, he talked to the doctor doing the test, but she was new to the Tim Dean approach. He knew what she was doing and why, and made no secret of his knowledge. If the cancer had spread to his bone marrow, his chances of recovery would be greatly reduced. His openness shook her and she seemed unsure how to continue the conversation; 'it was a bit like when you drop a clanger in a roomful of people and everyone falls silent.'

On the evening of Thursday 26 July he became feverish. The staff took his temperature every two hours; the thermometer was in a tube attached to the bed. As he felt himself getting hotter, he reached for it between official checks and stuck it in his mouth. It registered 103.5°F, and was rising. He knew that temperature was potentially dangerous. He pressed the bedside buzzer and called a nurse. She gave him the thermometer again; his reading was correct. She sent for the house doctor.

Nurses began to bathe Tim in ice-cold water. They had to be careful; if they lowered his temperature too quickly they could kill him rather than help him. After some time they reduced it by a full degree, and he felt less uncomfortable.

Then the doctors gave him the anti-cancer drugs. His condition was so bad that they could not afford to wait any longer before chemotherapy. If it was not now, it might be never.

The prayer meeting in Virginia Water was taking place at

the same time, its participants unaware of the dramatic turn of events.

The medical treatment of Hodgkin's Disease was still in its very early stages in 1973. Some drugs were known to be effective against it, but they were lethal toxins with brutal side-effects. Tim was injected with two drugs. One of them, Mustine, or nitrogen mustard, was the active component of the cruel first world war mustard gas which caused heavy blistering of the skin, and internal damage. It kills all living cells, but has a slight preference for cancerous ones. The other drug was Vincristine.

He was warned that he might have a metallic taste in his mouth, and that he might be sick during the night. Then he was given sleeping tablets and left alone. He had the metallic taste. He was sick, several times. He slept, off and on.

When he awoke on Friday morning, he felt much better. The Registrar, Dr Warenius, came to see him. He looked at Tim's neck. The lump had shrunk overnight from the size of a grapefruit to that of an inverted tablespoon.

The doctor got out his notepad and pen. He marked a small dot on the pad. 'If that dot represents millions of cells,' he said, 'just think what work has been done on the countless billions that were in the lump.'

Tim asked to get out of bed, but the request was refused until Saturday. His body needed time to adjust after running such a high temperature and having been blasted by powerful drugs. On Sunday he was allowed out of Greenhow Ward, to stroll around the hospital's labyrinthine corridors. And on Monday afternoon he was let out of the hospital itself. He took the underground to where Tony Wales lived, but he was out, so Tim sauntered back to the hospital in time for his evening meal.

On Tuesday he went for a walk down the nearby Charing Cross Road, lined with bookshops and leading to Nelson's Column and the fountains in Trafalgar Square, and the sun warmed him. He looked down at the pavement, watching himself put one foot in front of the other. 'And I'm thinking. "Isn't this amazing?" And I'm talking to God and saying, "Isn't this fantastic? I'm actually able to walk!" '

From his head to his heart flowed the thrill of a fresh discovery. He had known it but never before had he felt it so powerfully. 'Isn't the human body incredible in the way it functions!' It was good, so good, to be alive!

If miracles can ever be compared, it was impossible to tell which was the greater: the gift of life, or its restoration.

For you created my inmost being:
   you knit me together in my mother's womb.
I praise you because I am fearfully and wonderfully made;
   your works are wonderful,
   I know that full well.
My frame was not hidden from you
   when I was made in the secret place.
When I was woven together in the depths of the earth,
   your eyes saw my unformed body.
All the days ordained for me
   were written in your book
   before one of them came to be.
How precious to me are your thoughts, O God!
   How vast is the sum of them!
Were I to count them,
   they would outnumber the grains of sand,
When I awake,
   I am still with you (Psalm 139:13–18).

So rapid was his recovery that one new patient in the ward indignantly complained to another, 'What's the matter with him? What's he taking up a valuable bed for?'

He was told to shut up. 'Last week he couldn't even walk,' said the other.

About a week later Dr Jelliffe came round the ward, leading a group of visiting Asian doctors. He stopped by Tim's bed; Tim had been sent back to it pending the visit. 'Well, Timothy, I understand you're doing rather well,' Dr Jelliffe said.

He sat on the side of the bed, put his right hand to Tim's neck, parting the hair. As he looked and felt, he jerked back with surprise. Then he sighed, 'We should have photographed this.' Properly documented and illustrated, it could have reached the medical journals, if not the next revision of the textbooks. With more excitement in his voice than he usually permitted, he explained to the visitors what had happened.

On Friday 3 August Tim was discharged from hospital, less than two weeks after he had been admitted as an emergency case. The treatment was not yet complete and the Hodgkin's Disease saga was by no means over; Agatha Christie herself could not have devised so many twists to a tale.

But it was time to return to a relatively normal life, and to prepare to join the IVF staff as arts students travelling secretary.

And to reflect on questions which had never been far from his mind; questions which formed the standard raw material for student discussions but which, for Tim, had ceased to be merely intellectual, and had become instead intensely practical and personal.

Ten

Questions in search of answers

When Tim's sister Verity first heard the news that he had cancer, her reaction was, 'He's too young and innocent to die.' Not that Tim was a paragon of virtue in her eyes, but it was the natural reaction many people feel when faced with what seems to be undeserved suffering. We almost instinctively associate suffering with divine punishment, and our natural sense of justice rebels against what seems to be excessive retribution.

It was an issue which Tim was not afraid to face. He was as honest as a human being can be; 'If my cancer was caused by something I'd done, then I had to find out what it was.' He did not expect to be left in the dark. 'I don't believe that God is someone who, once the question is genuinely asked, wishes to torture someone. God is not a torturer. So unless he gives a clear answer and points out something that's wrong, forget it.'

He was well aware that St Paul had told the disorderly and schismatic Corinthian Christians that their spiritual hypocrisy and carelessness over the true meaning of the holy communion service, attendance at which made little or no difference to their selfish behaviour in a city renowned for its moral licence, had led to personal suffering and illness. 'This is why many among you are weak and sick, and a number of you have fallen asleep (died)' (1 Cor. 11:20).

If it happened then, it could happen again, Tim reasoned. 'Occasionally some afflictions may be a specific rebuke from God, but that is probably exceedingly rare.

And it is a sub-clause in the overriding principle that suffering is not normally the result of personal sin.' That gives no support to the person who is ever eager to point the finger of accusation at another; ninety-nine times out of a hundred they will be wrong. Tim was not alone, however, among Christian sufferers to have to face the accusation that his cancer was a result of his sin, made by a well-meaning but misguided person whose beliefs could only add to the burden he already had to bear.

His grounds for believing that such a link between personal sin and suffering was rare was based on his understanding of the book of Job, in which the issue had been debated at length. Job was a wealthy, righteous man who lost all his children and possessions, and was afflicted with a loathsome, probably stress-related skin disease. The theology of his day sent people scuttling to the moral account books the moment anyone suffered, to find the discrepancies which had apparently displeased the Divine Auditor. So when Job's three friends came to visit him, they began to suggest that he needed to repent of some evil deed or thought. Against their advice, however, he maintained his innocence to the end.

Job eventually received an answer from God – in the form of a rebuke. It was not a rebuke for wrong actions; he was never forced by a Great Inquisitor to confess to sins he had never committed. Rather, it was a rebuke for having expected to understand the mysteries of the universe, and for justifying himself at the expense of God's reputation for justice.

> Where were you when I laid the earth's foundation?
>   Tell me, if you understand.
> Who marked off its dimensions? Surely you know!
>   Who stretched a measuring line across it?
> On what were its footings set,
>   or who laid its cornerstone –
> while the morning stars sang together
>   and all the angels shouted for joy? (Job 38: 4–7)

It provided a reassuring thought for Tim, even if it did not provide a full intellectual answer to his questions. 'The answer God gave to Job is that "I am so great that you can't fathom it". There's a mystery there, and there's no way we will fully comprehend it. But he does give us concrete ways to get into it. For example, suffering is rooted in "the fall".'

All suffering, Tim reasoned, was evil: there was nothing intrinsically good about it, however much good might come from it. And evil had entered the world through the sinfulness of mankind. 'I don't think we can keep crying at God and calling him a rotten so-and-so because he's doing all these bad things. That attitude fundamentally undermines the fact that sin and suffering are related to the fall, to mankind as a whole being out of a true relationship with God.'

The problem arises most acutely for those who believe that God is good. If we are the hapless victims of some perverse spiritual joke, or if we are caught in the cross-fire between two equal, opposite and eternal spiritual forces forever slugging out their power struggle and commandeering the earth as their battleground (as some other religions have suggested), then there is no 'problem'; there is no hope and no help for us, and despair is the only logical response. But the Christian faith begins with a good God and a perfect creation and ends with a good God and a perfect new creation. So what has happened in the middle?

All we are told in the Bible is that back in the ghostly mists of pre-history something went terribly wrong with the physical expression of God's perfection. In a catastrophe of huge magnitude, like that of a massive earthquake which changes the face of a whole landscape, the world was shaken out of its original moral and spiritual alignment, and the effects were felt through the whole of creation. Mankind had announced his arrival on earth by trespassing thoughtlessly on holy ground, and by trampling carelessly over the maker's instructions in his rush to prove that he was now in charge. He flew in the face of pure Love, and felt the full force of its righteous indignation:

Cursed is the ground because of you;
　　through painful toil you will eat of it
　　all the days of your life.
It will produce thorns and thistles for you . . .
By the sweat of your brow
　　you will eat your food
until you return to the ground,
　　since from it you were taken;
for dust you are
　　and to dust you will return (Gen. 3:17–19).

The earth trembled. Delicately balanced processes were torn apart; natural harmonies became discordant. Seeds of chaos were sown which would multiply in pain, suffering, disorder and death. Estranged from his creator by a spiritual separation so profound that it was itself called 'death', man was destined to wander over the face of the once-friendly earth and to find that it was now less hospitable, malicious even, and that his own powers to subdue it were diminished. Now instead of coaxing it, he would be battling against it; instead of controlling it, he would be constantly frustrated by it; instead of living in harmony with his fellow creatures, he would be suspicious of them and threatened by them.

Precisely how diseases, and the 'natural' disasters of earthquake, flood and tempest, fit into that unhappy scene we are not directly told. The biblical picture of 'the fall' is impressionistic, not photographic, capturing the sense but not the science. However it is a matter of observable fact that a great deal of human suffering is man-made anyway. It is not a matter of an angry God inflicting divine retribution on a rebellious world so much as that rebellious world stewing in its own juice. Greed, hatred, envy, malice, jealousy, lust, and pride all have their roots in the fall of man, and their fruits in the wars, thefts, feuds and failed promises which wound bodies, divide communities and break hearts.

So, Tim reasoned, perhaps there was a sense in which his

cancer (and all other such 'undeserved' illnesses) might be somehow bound up with human sinfulness in general, without being tied to an individual's specific wrong-doing. 'We do not know to what extent humanity is responsible for the many diseases we get. It may be revealed to us eventually that many of the complaints we have are far more due to humanity's mismanagement than to any sense of divine retribution. We don't know why cancer starts, although there are clues; stress and diet sometimes may have something to do with it. And if suffering is a part of humanity's mismanagement, then we have to take steps to get it back in order again.'

Years later, Tim was to quote with approval an article from *The Economist* on the famine which ravaged Ethiopia: 'It takes acts of men to turn acts of God into calamity.'[1]

His conclusion was borne out by two incidents in the gospels. On one occasion Jesus was faced by a blind man, and his disciples asked, 'Who sinned, this man or his parents, that he was born blind?'

Jesus would have none of it: 'Neither this man nor his parents sinned, but this happened so that the work of God might be displayed in his life' (John 9:2–3). On another occasion Jesus took the initiative himself. There had been a massacre at a religious festival. The worshippers had been mown down in cold blood by power-crazed soldiers acting on the orders of a tyrannical Roman procurator. Jesus asked: 'Do you think that these Galileans were worse sinners than all the other Galileans because they suffered in this way?' And he answered his own question: 'I tell you, no. But unless you repent, you too will all perish' (Luke 13:1–5).

In other words, it is a fact that some overtly wicked people appear to escape God's notice entirely and prosper from their greed or crime. It is also a fact of life that some saintly people appear only to get a kick in the teeth for all their goodness. There is often no discernible pattern of cause and effect because there was never meant to be any such pattern. The world God made is not ruled by the rough justice of a savage school playground, where blow is exchanged for blow. It is a fallen world, and suffering is for that very reason often arbitrary and unjust.

He who searches for specific rhyme or reason for confusing and apparently random afflictions is often forced to agree with the sad conclusion of the biblical sage:

> The race is not to the swift
>   or the battle to the strong,
> nor does food come to the wise
>   or wealth to the brilliant
>   or favour to the learned;
> but time and chance happen to them all (Eccles. 9:11).

So Tim examined himself before God and while he found the exercise helpful as a personal spiritual discipline, 'I concluded that God was saying that personal sin had nothing to do directly with my illness. What I was experiencing was something to do with the fact that all humanity shares in the sufferings which are the result of mankind's departure from God.'

He could not have been accused of being a lukewarm Christian. Unwise, perhaps, in his sometimes confrontational approach to people; over-assertive, perhaps, of his deeply-held beliefs; over-eager, perhaps, in his celebration of freedom from the scruples which bound other Christians. But not lukewarm, just growing up; not exceptionally sinful, just human.

That meant that the proper question for him to ask was not, 'Why should I suffer?' but 'Why should I *not* suffer?' This was further clarified for him some months later when he read a book which he was to rave about at student conferences whenever he had the chance; at one conference he got up at every point when announcements were made and added some brief comment about John Wenham's *The Goodness of God* (now re-issued as *The Enigma of Evil*); some 200 copies were sold in three days to about 300 students. In the book, Wenham points out that 'any apparent unfairness in God's treatment of us arises not because some have too much punishment, but because some of us appear to have too little.'[2] He who takes sin seriously knows that the slightest deviation from God's norms is an affront to him.

Indeed, when he considered the fact that 'God can let his Son go through suffering beyond what we can imagine for an overriding good purpose, then that could also happen to us in some smaller way.' If Jesus was not exempt from suffering, why, he reasoned, should we expect to be?

Not only did Jesus endure the horrific torture of the physical crucifixion, one of mankind's nastiest forms of execution. In some unimaginable way he also carried in his unique personality the guilt and eternal consequences of human sinfulness, so that the broken love-relationship between God and man could be repaired. And if that is dismissed as being too unique for it to be a precedent for continued suffering among his followers, there is always his childhood poverty, later homelessness and hunger, and the emotional stress of Gethsemane, to illustrate the fact that his daily life was not clothed in satin nor cushioned by cottonwool.

His sufferings can rarely be compared favourably with ours; they were more intense. For Tim, that provided both a comfort and a challenge. It was a comfort because 'the reason I can have confidence in Jesus Christ is that he did not walk around three feet above the ground, but because I know that he knows what suffering is like. He's gone through it.'

And it was a challenge because 'once, when I felt very sorry for myself, I had to say that my sufferings are nothing compared with his.' That is not, of course, a fact to be held insensitively against others who are feeling the full force of their infirmity. He hurts with those who hurt, even if their experience is somehow less than his. Tim's experience of intense pain had reminded him that sufferings cannot be fully compared like examination papers. One person's pain threshold is very different to another's. And what may seem unbearable to our imagination may be (just) bearable in the event.

So, like Jesus, the Church is 'incarnate' in the world, its eternal life clothed with frail flesh. That, Tim realised, is essential to its ministry. 'One of the great wisdoms of God is that we are redeemed yet remain fallen until Christ comes again. That gives us our total solidarity with mankind, and we are afflicted by the evil of the world and we share in its sufferings. In fact, it's important for the Church to suffer as humanity does, just as Christ suffered in the world. It would be horrific if we were immune; we could not identify at all with those who suffer.'

That does not mean – as some sections of the Church have taught – that a Christian is incomplete unless he or she has suffered. 'I do not believe in the sanctity of suffering.' Tim did realise, however, that 'suffering may be part of our discipleship – just as it was for Jesus.' And with that broad perspective which Christian faith brings, he was able to take comfort from the fact that the fallen creation shall one day be renewed, and disease shall be a thing of the past:

> Then I saw a new heaven and a new earth . . . And I heard a loud voice from the throne saying, 'Now the dwelling of God is with men, and he will live with them. They will be his people, and God himself will be with them and be their God. He will wipe every tear from their eyes. There will be no more death or mourning or crying or pain, for the old order of things has passed away' (Rev. 21:1, 3, 4).

In the meantime, God's promise is to walk with his people through the valley of dark sufferings, a promise Tim had believed before he was ill, which he had found true already in his two months in hospital, and which he was to prove true again in the months to come.

To those Christians who in their enthusiasm for healing looked for swift and non-medical cures, Tim pointed out that even St Paul, with his healing gift, had to leave his friend Trophimus ill in Miletus. Indeed, those who are healed have to suffer first, before they receive the cure. As he wrestled with these issues, Tim coined the epithet, 'Unless you have a theology of suffering to go with your theology of healing, your theology is unbalanced.'

The question of healing was to become more important for him at a later stage. At this point, his neck had been reduced to near normal size, and he felt well in himself. But he was not yet healed.

And there were some more traumas to come.

Eleven

A new beginning

Tim was raring to go. He had been largely inactive for nearly three months and under-employed for eighteen. Dr Oliver Barclay, then IVF General Secretary, advised him to take it easy for the first term of his job as arts students travelling secretary. 'Don't worry if you don't do any work for three months,' he said.

It was a kind and thoughtful gesture, although not advice which Tim was likely to heed. But he was impressed by it, and by the fact that the IVF had stood by him during his illness. While there was no other candidate competing for his job, the senior staff knew that taking a cancer patient on the payroll was not without its risks – although they rarely considered them. Tim was the right man for the job, and the future was entirely in God's hands. The fact had been an important morale booster for him as he lay in hospital; it gave him hope, something to look forward to.

There had been a degree of caution on both sides. During one informal interview with Dr Barclay, Tim bought a half-pint of lager simply to make a point about his way of life. The next interview was over a hamburger in a (dry) cafe when the responsibilities of the job in terms of pastoral care and personal discipline were made clear to him. He had no desire to present a false image, but he accepted the responsibility neither to cause young Christians unnecessary offence nor to place 'stumbling blocks' in their way. A number of his friends were encouraging him to take the job, and after several interviews and much thought and prayer, he was formally offered it, and accepted it, much to the excitement and relief of the IVF as well as Tim himself.

So on Friday 31 August 1973 he caught the Inter-City train from London, to travel to the large but isolated conference centre at the village of Swanwick in Derbyshire. Purpose-built round a country house, the centre had once been a prisoner of war camp. In the years which followed, its blocks of tiny rooms had been modernised and extended, and 'Swanwick' had become (and remains) a substitute word for 'conference' in the vocabulary of many Christian students – and indeed many other organisations unconnected with the IVF. Tim went there for the ICCF* leadership conference, to meet for the first time both his new colleagues on the staff and some of the students he would be helping and advising in the future. But he was not feeling 100 per cent well.

The night before, he had been back in hospital. Although the Hodgkin's Disease appeared to have retreated, he still needed chemotherapy to ensure it was destroyed completely. And one of the drugs had the side-effects he had already experienced. The Mustine had a metallic taste and later made him sick, sometimes several times, in the night. For twenty-four hours after the monthly dose of Mustine and Vincristine he felt drained and below par, suffering from flu. The sleeping and anti-sickness pills had only a minor palliative effect. A week or so later he was given another dose of Vincristine and the booster drugs Prednisone and Procarbozine, which did not have any adverse effects. The regime (usually known to the medical staff as MOPP – the drugs had alternative names) was in its early stages. It had provided a breakthrough in the treat-

*ICCF – the Inter-College Christian Fellowship – was the name of the technical colleges' and polytechnics' department of IVF, within which Tim functioned. It merged in 1976 (just after Tim had left) with the Colleges of Education Christian Union (CECU) to form a single Colleges Department, as by then many of the staff and some of the activities embraced all non-university colleges. IVF changed its name to UCCF – Universities and Colleges Christian Fellowship – in 1975.

ment of Hodgkin's patients a couple of years before Tim developed the illness, but compared with the advances made since 1973 the treatment was relatively crude, and the side-effects were excessive.

Chemotherapy made life frustrating, as well as regularly unpleasant. Tim had to plan his diary around his visits to the Middlesex for the drugs, and rule out of his diary the evening of the first dose and most of the next day. In a job which involved travel nationwide and which had to be tailored to fit the timetables of colleges and advance plans of Christian Unions, this fact was a source of irritation to him. Above all, it contradicted the one revered aim of medical care. Most people go to hospital in the hope that they will be made well. Tim, now feeling perfectly well and with no medical evidence of disease, faced monthly visits to hospital in order to be made horrendously ill. The prospect was as unpleasant as the result. He began shaking and sweating the moment he stepped on the underground train to travel to the hospital. He decided that he could not face it and, rather boldly, after the late August dose asked to be taken off the drugs. Dr Jelliffe was understanding, but firm.

18 September 1973

Dear Tim,

Thank you for your letter. I was delighted that you yourself think you are doing well. I know you are doing well but it is always cheering when I know that a patient also feels confident about his progress.

I think it is extremely unlikely that we shall find any active disease even if we open you up again. (Don't worry, this is not part of the programme.) However, I would be against stopping your treatment at the moment even though I realise the drugs we use are fairly strong and produce temporary upset which is quite considerable. In our experience if we do not continue with the drugs for a reasonable period of time after the disease is controlled, then recurrence is more likely. If there is further trouble it may be necessary to start right at the beginning again and this obviously is a waste of time from the patient's point of view. As soon as I think it is safe to stop I shall say so. I sympathise with your point of view as I do not like being hurt or made sick myself.

Kindest regards
Yours sincerely,
A.M. Jelliffe, MD, FRCP, FFR.

Tim saw the sense of it. God, he believed, had healed him in a quite remarkable fashion. But, he reasoned, that did not give him the right to fly in the face of common sense, nor to disregard the proven experience of the doctors. His stewardship of his newly-regained health required that he take the necessary precautions to avoid falling prey to the disease again. He submitted to further doses of chemotherapy, and the inconvenience they caused.

Meanwhile, he was having some fun as well. He found that his fellow travelling secretaries were people he could relate to easily and comfortably. One in particular, Phil Hill, he got to know well after sitting next to him at the new staff induction course in September. Unknown to most other people (Tim included) in the IVF boardroom in Bedford Square, London, we had set Phil Hill up as a devil's advocate during a session on student leadership. It was a hallowed principle of the IVF that each Christian Union should be autonomous and that its leadership should remain entirely in the students' hands; the staff were merely advisors and supporters.

It was clearly a principle fraught with potential dangers, but adhered to with good reason. It did not take much imagination to think of arguments against it and of possible troubles which might arise from it. And Phil had both a good imagination and a strong Welsh accent, with the direct manner and eloquent speech which often accompanies them. He launched into an invective against student

leadership in order to make the other new staff think and
talk through the principle. However, he did it so well that
he almost convinced Oliver Barclay (who had not been
warned in advance) that he had made a grave mistake in
appointing him. Tim, sitting next to Phil, could almost feel
the heat rising, and could sense Phil's growing discomfort
as Dr Barclay remonstrated with him. It was the kind of
situation Tim enjoyed, and it endeared him to his neighbour.

The early days at IVF were learning days for Tim. He
had had little to do with Christian Unions when he had
been a student, and so was unfamiliar with the organisational aspects, even though he was full of ideas about
relating his faith to the arts. So to initiate him into the job
(as well as to compensate for the fact that he could not yet
drive, and to introduce him to as wide a range of students as
possible) he spent several days at a time travelling with
other staff members.

One was Bob Cutler, whose 'parish' covered the whole
of the east and west Midlands conurbations, and who later
pioneered Christian work among students overseas. He
taught Tim the effective trick of literally tipping a cardboard box of books out on the floor and encouraging the
students to rummage through them; they seemed to buy
more that way than if the books were neatly displayed on
wire stands. Tim later found himself a plastic crate to use as
his book hold-all.

Bob Cutler also asked Tim, at short notice, to give an
evangelistic talk at a polytechnic CU on 'Is there life before
death?' (the title was taken from some well-known 1960s
graffiti). He had never preached a sermon in his life, and
although he had given talks and lectures, he had never
given one specifically to encourage people to become
Christians. He took a text from Ephesians on the theme of
alienation: 'And you he made alive, when you were dead
through the trespasses and sins in which you once walked'
(Eph. 2:5, RSV).

Despite his normal verbal fluency, he dried up after only

fifteen minutes; he had no idea how to round the talk off, and Bob stepped in to rescue him and to conclude the meeting. Tim slunk into a corner; he felt embarrassed. He had failed; he had let the Christian Union down – the members had invited their non-Christian friends to come specially to the meeting. No one came over to speak to him, not even out of courtesy.

When most people had left, a black girl approached him. She was crying. 'No one has ever recognised before that I'm dead inside,' she sobbed.

His abysmally-presented message had got through to at least one person. He handed her over to a responsible Christian student for further counselling. It was another reminder that God was not wasting his time, even in the morass of human weakness.

Being forced to travel long distances by train gave him a unique opportunity to read widely and to spend time preparing talks, some of which would be given many times over in different contexts. The experience of his first speaking engagement was not to be repeated.

But the experience of chemotherapy was repeated for several months to come. Then with the dawn of 1974 there came sweet release from six hellish months. His remission, in medical terms, had been extremely rapid. At the end of January Dr Jelliffe kept his word; he stopped the drugs. Now Tim could work without the rude interruption of treatment. He could put the past behind him. For a short while.

Twelve

Into the valley of darkness

Tim had a new home. When the ceiling had crashed in on him at the Highbury Park flat, after he had left hospital, he knew the time had come to move. From September to December 1973 he had lodged temporarily with Norman Stone, journalist and poet Steve Turner, and architect Ray Hall in part of the building in Buckingham Palace Road (near the Victoria railway and bus stations) which had once been the offices of *Hansard*, the daily record of Britain's parliamentary debates.

In January 1974 he found a two storey house in Cholmeley Park, a tree-lined road in north London, which was available for rental. It would accommodate eight people, whose combined resources would be needed to pay the rent. The IVF lent him £150 for the deposit, on condition that the sleeping accommodation was split into two halves, with the men on one floor and the women on another. Tony Hudson and Malcolm Doney shared a large downstairs room, and Tim had a small one to himself. Five women shared three top floor bedrooms, where there was also an enormous communal lounge and the kitchen.

Cholmeley Park took over where the Muswell Hill Road flat had left off twelve months before; it became something of a social centre. On one occasion (and remarkably, only on one occasion) when Tim arrived home in the early hours of the morning after visiting a college Christian Union, he crept into his room only to find a strange woman in his bed. Although he had told the other occupants of the house that he would be back that night, as he had not arrived by the late evening they assumed he was not coming and gave his room to their visitor.

On Tuesday 12 March 1974 Tim was alone in his room. It was about six-thirty in the evening, and he was sitting in an armchair reading a book. It was Jim Packer's *Evangelism and the sovereignty of God*, addressing an age-old controversy within the Church.

> God's sovereignty and man's responsibility are taught us side by side in the same Bible; sometimes, indeed, in the same text. Both are thus guaranteed to us by the same divine authority; both, therefore, are true. It follows that they must be held together, and not played off against each other. Man is a responsible moral agent, though he is *also* divinely controlled; man is divinely controlled, though he is *also* a responsible moral agent. God's sovereignty is a reality, and man's responsibility is a reality too.[1]

It was a book which had greatly influenced Tim's thinking some years before. In his early student days he had been a strong advocate of only one side of this truth, emphasising the freedom of choice with which God had endowed the human race. But after reading Packer, among other books, he had been persuaded that such an exclusive emphasis almost made man the author of his own salvation. He realised that God's kingship (or sovereignty) was active in individuals as he guided them towards faith, as well as in their later Christian lives as he worked out his purposes through them. God was not just the titular king of an indifferent province; he was the ruler of human affairs, and the active head of the Church.

A good book is always worth reading more than once, and Tim had returned to Packer; despite his apparently disastrous first effort back in September, he was encouraging students to share the gospel with others as part of his work, and Packer provided raw material for talks on the subject.

Tim's hands and slender fingers are rarely still – the outward sign of an active and creative mind. He had a habit, as he read, of stroking his beard. He was doing just that on the evening of 12 March.

Suddenly his fingers stopped in mid-stroke; his concentration switched abruptly from the book to his neck. He had touched a lump which should not have been there. It was the size of a peanut. And it was hard; if it had been merely an enlarged lymph node going about its lawful business of exterminating microbiological invaders it would have been more pulpy.

He had no doubts. He knew instantly that Hodgkin's Disease had recurred. For a moment it seemed as if the world had stopped spinning – just when it appeared to have picked up momentum. Quite apart from the worrying fact of having cancer itself, he would have to go through the nauseous business of chemotherapy all over again. It was a stunning blow. He went into the next room; Tony Hudson was there and he told him the news.

The next day he visited his doctor, who referred him back to the Middlesex Hospital. He gave Tim a letter which he took in on the Thursday. On Sunday, after attending his church, St Helen's Bishopsgate in the heart of the City of London's banking and commercial district, he went across to All Souls Langham Place (then meeting at St Peter's Vere Street during alterations). He knew that Oliver Barclay, the IVF General Secretary, worshipped there; he wanted to break the news to him personally rather than over the phone.

They met in the warm sunshine outside; Tim half expected to have his contract discontinued, but the concern and support he had been given before had not been exhausted.

This time he had to wait over a month for the biopsy, staying in the hospital for a couple of days towards the end of April. Then another month elapsed before the dreaded drug treatment began. No surgical operation was required this time. The disease was not advanced; it was only in one part of his body, and there was less need for hasty treatment.

He asked Dr Jelliffe whether the drugs would be worse than the previous ones. The Consultant was tactful but guarded. 'No, I don't think so,' he said. It was barely the truth, but for once Tim was glad that he was not forewarned. He might not have turned up for the first appointment.

With the disease having returned so soon, it was highly likely that he would die. As a result, the doctors decided to try a new drug on him, CCNU. It had been developed at the Hammersmith Hospital in west London for treating leukaemia patients, and it was being tried on eleven Hodgkin's patients at the Middlesex Hospital as well. The drug was still only on clinical trial and had not been licensed for general use; each batch had to be sent to the Middlesex from Hammersmith clearly marked with the designated patient's name.

The treatment began on Monday 24 May; it was always to be a Monday. Each time he presented himself at the hospital and was sent to whatever ward had a spare bed. (He once went into the ward which treated skin diseases and discovered that the sheets on the beds were green.) He was injected with Bleomycin, a thick ooze which took a painfully long time to drain from the syringe into his buttock, and Vinblastine. Then he was given ten pills to swallow. Five of them made up the new drug, CCNU. Two were anti-emetics to control the inevitable sickness, and three were sleeping pills to relax him and try to reduce his awareness of the side-effects.

The five palliatives seemed to have little effect; Tim was dragged through a hell hotter than he had dared imagine. Once again the drugs made him violently sick, frequently, until he got to the worst point of all; his body had nothing more to eject yet kept on trying to do so all the same. He feared that all his organs were about to discharge from their rightful places. The next day, he felt smashed to pieces; he was in no fit state to do anything. And as in the previous course of treatment, this was followed by a bout of twenty-four hour flu. A week later he returned to the hospital as an outpatient for a follow-up injection, which mercifully had no noticable side-effect on him, and he could go straight home afterwards.

He had no outward symptoms of Hodgkin's Disease. He had no night sweats, and he was not even feeling tired or run down; he felt perfectly well. Yet once a month he had to swallow poison and suffer the consequences. He had to voluntarily submit to chemical torture, and he was not a masochist.

Tim had read a number of war books, and he knew all about the tortures inflicted in certain prisoner of war and concentration camps. 'I had always thought that if I was ever subject to torture I would not be able to withstand it.'

His belief began to look prophetic. The sense of dread and unease grew as he travelled to the hospital. The pills became increasingly difficult to swallow. He struggled through three courses of treatment.

Then on 19 August he entered hospital for the fourth. He vomited the pills out seconds after he had swallowed them. Physically and psychologically, he had had enough. He apologised to the nurse. 'Look, I'm terribly sorry. It's not your fault, but there's no way I can take these drugs.' His body and his mind had been crushed by the torture. He had collapsed. And then the fears rushed in, like debris being sucked into a vacuum. He knew that if he did not take the drugs, the Hodgkin's Disease would get worse and that he could die. He also knew that he could not take the drugs again. His depression grew deep.

He was kept in hospital for a couple of days this time, and the treatment was discontinued. You can lead a horse to water, but you cannot force it to drink. His phobia was so bad that when he took one of the women living at the Cholmeley Park house to see Francois Truffaut's film *Day for Night*, he had to avert his eyes from the screen when a huge pill was projected onto it.

Then an American lady stepped into his life. She was a

clinical psychologist at the Middlesex whose job it was to help him overcome his aversion. And with her came another of those little signs that the God he trusted was still working 'in all things . . . for the good of those who love him' (Rom. 8:28). She lived in the same road as Tim. That was no passing coincidence; it was to have a practical consequence.

He visited her regularly at the hospital. She used a simple bio-feedback machine, a black box attached by leads to his fingers, which measured the level of sweat. If he was tense, his hands perspired, and the machine emitted a high-pitched whine. As he relaxed, there was less sweat, and the whine was reduced to an intermittent bleep. The machine had seven settings; the idea was to get it down to a slow bleep on the lowest, most sensitive setting.

The psychologist taught him relaxation exercises and when he got the machine to bleep, she gave him a small pill-shaped sweet and told him to swallow it. Then she turned the machine to its next setting, and began the exercise all over again. After several sessions, he felt relaxed enough to swallow the sweet without sending the machine into a squealing fit.

By October, he was ready to try the chemotherapy once more. The treatment had to begin all over again; he faced a full six month course. The American psychologist volunteered to come with him; their relationship had progressed a little beyond the clinical. She had even been introduced to the mysteries of English soccer by accompanying Tim and friends to watch West Ham. Her efforts went far beyond her call of duty, and were made outside her normal working hours; the drugs were always administered at night to reduce the after-effects. But it was extremely reassuring for Tim to have her beside him, as he coaxed her machine down to a gentle bleep and swallowed the pills as quickly as he could.

Over the intervening months he had also kept in contact with David, the hospital pharmacist who had spied the books on French film-maker Jean Luc Godard when Tim had first arrived at the Middlesex the previous year. David was aware of Tim's traumas and offered some help of his own.

'Tell me what day you are coming in,' he said. 'I can intercept your drugs when they arrive from Hammersmith. Then I'll turn the five CCNU pills into two capsules; you'll have three less to swallow.'

That was good news indeed. But it was not the end of David's helpful ideas. 'Why do you stay in hospital for the drugs?' he asked. 'You've got to come in for the injection. But why not go home and take the pills there? Have some friends round, and cook a really good meal. You'll have pleasant company, and you'll fill your stomach. Before you sit down to eat, take the sleeping pills. You'll get drowsy and after about forty-five minutes you'll have to leave the dinner. Then take your CCNU and go to bed.'

So he did. And he invited the clinical psychologist, who lived in the same road, to come too. She did, bringing her machine with her. One of the women in the house cooked a good meal. When it was over, Tim was already feeling sleepy. He went to his room, used the machine to relax still further, took the drugs, and fell asleep almost at once.

He woke up in the night to be sick, using a bowl he had placed at his bedside; he was too drowsy to get up. It was a waste of good food, but a far less painful experience than in the past. When he awoke the next day, not until early afternoon, the bowl was gone. In its place was another – full of cornflakes. One of his fellow tenants had acted as a ministering angel. 'That was a horrible task for someone. But that's what friends are all about.'

It hardly made the treatment pleasant; he was still shattered the next day and he still had his flu symptoms. But it made it bearable.

In January 1975, he sent out his termly newsletter to the many individuals who prayed for him and his work.

Dr Jelliffe has said he can find no trace of Hodgkin's in me but he wishes me to continue treatment for at least three

*months to really try and severely diminish the prospect of
another recurrence. I mention this not as a plea for undue
attention and sympathy, but honestly to express my very
real need for your prayers over this aspect of my life.*

*It would be great to put on a broad smile and say with
vain piety that I count it all joy every time I have treatment.
For anything up to two weeks in every month a physical
depression leading to an emotional depression has led me
into distorted thinking about life, and this must have
affected my ministry.*

His depressions had been serious, although not totally
debilitating. Depression had been within the compass of his
experience since childhood, although since his commitment to Christ he had never suffered from the black hope-
lessness which had occasionally invaded his mind before.
But during the chemotherapy his emotions had been hit
almost as hard, it seemed, as his body. He felt flattened,
and just when he needed him most God seemed a million
miles away. It would have been bad enough in any circumstances, but when he had to speak about God and encourage others in their spiritual development, it became a
huge strain.

It helped when he realised that the depressions were
drug-induced. The connection between his physical and his
psychological well-being was far closer than he had
previously believed. Physical illness and pain, surgical
operations and drugs, the strange unnatural environment
of a hospital ward: these things can play havoc with the
emotions of the most balanced person. And that taught
Tim something fresh about the reality of God.

'You can't base your relationship with God on your own
feelings. If you did, you'd conclude that most of the time
God is far away. The opposite is true. God's closeness to
me, and his caring for me, does not depend on my
emotional state. I could come out of a depression and know
that God was with me even though I couldn't perceive it.
It's amazing how insidious the temptation is in such circum-

stances to judge your spiritual state entirely on your feelings.'

The biblical promise stands secure and unbroken: 'I will never leave you or forsake you.' But the human experience of devastating aloneness was not even denied the Son of God: 'My God, my God, why have you forsaken me?' (Josh. 1:5; Matt. 27:46). From October 1974 to March 1975 Tim Dean learnt the force of both in a new way. And he could truthfully say with the psalmist:

> If I go up to the heavens, you are there;
> If I make my bed in the depths, you are there . . .
> even the darkness will not be dark to you;
> the night will shine like the day,
> for darkness is as light to you (Ps. 139:8, 12).

By then, Hodgkin's Disease was in complete remission. The fact that it could theoretically recur yet again hardly entered his mind; rightly so. He was given a daily maintaining drug as a medical precaution against an early relapse. It had no side-effects.

It was all over. For nearly two years his life had been dominated by disease and drugs; now he was released from their shackles. He had shared in humanity's sufferings in an unenviable and horrendous manner. He had been healed.

And when he looked back over the experience, he could dimly perceive something of the connection between faith and medicine, and the fact that even in his extremity, God had a good plan and purpose.

Which was more than one sincere but mistaken person could understand . . .

Thirteen

Tracing the rainbow

Just after he had the operation to remove his spleen, and before he was rushed back to hospital for chemotherapy, Tim had received some advice in a letter.

> *Dear Tim,*
>
> *Although we hardly know each other, from the moment I learned of your illness you've been on my heart and in my prayers.*
>
> *Humanly speaking as you must know, the prognosis is not good. I know that you need a miracle BEFORE the doctors start their dangerous, poisonous and destructive 'treatments'.*
>
> *I'm told you would not consider going to a public healing meeting, Tim, yet this might be the very way in which God wants to glorify Himself through you.*
>
> *To be healed privately at home, or through the desperate ministrations of doctors in hospital, does not give God much glory. How much do you want to glorify the Lord? Even to the extent of all your pride?*
>
> *Time is short Tim; fast and pray. May God make you desperate – for His glory alone.*

It was hardly the most tactful approach, although Tim was spared the fate of some others in his position and received few such suggestions. Pride was not his greatest problem when he was crippled with pain. The doctors displayed no signs of being desperate, even if they were trawling in relatively uncharted waters. And Tim was concerned that

God should have due honour in his life. But through his two
years of illness he became further convinced that the
dichotomy driven between the prayer of faith and the
labour of doctors was false.

'I have no problem in believing that God can heal outside
all the normal practices of medicine. I would always ask for
that – I am not afraid to ask God for something which is
good. But I in no way believe that one can make demands
on God or indeed know what God will do.'

That was neither to deny the power of prayer, nor to
display ingratitude towards the doctors. Tim was convinced
that God had made him better, and that he had used both
prayer and medicine. No person on earth can plot or
predict God's methods as if they were moves on a chess
board, or stages in an experiment, and say with final
authority, that is how he did it, or how he will do it again.
The tapestry of God's handiwork comprises many closely-
woven threads; the temptation to human minds is to un-
ravel a couple of them and then confuse the tangled skein
for the complete pattern.

For the entire period of his illness, Tim was surrounded
by a great deal of loving prayer. The emergency prayer
meeting which was arranged before his re-admission to
hospital and also coincided with the first drug dose was an
outstanding but not isolated example. People and churches
around the country prayed for him. Some he had never
heard of, and learned only later of their concern; he had a
wide network of friends who were attached to an even
wider grapevine.

On two occasions Tim also sought public prayer for
healing accompanied by the traditional sign of fellowship,
the laying on of hands. Two of us from the IVF staff took
him to St Andrew's Church, Chorleywood, in Hertford-
shire, which then had a growing healing ministry. We
joined with the church leaders in praying specifically for his
healing, during a communion service. On another
occasion, after the recurrence of the disease, the senior
IVF staff gathered in the office boardroom to pray simi-

larly. On both occasions it seemed to Tim and to others to be utterly appropriate and right.

In the first instance he was opening himself to the spiritual gifts which God has given to the Church. It is the whole Church, and not simply gifted individuals within it, which ministers to the special needs of its members. Those with particular gifts exercise them as part of the whole Church's activity, and not as private individuals. Healing in particular is sometimes narrowed down to a one-to-one ministry, the gifted person aiding the needy person to get better – wrongly so, in Tim's view. 'Healing is not always seen as being part of a greater whole. What is a person healed for? In order to get back into Christian discipleship with its emphasis on the corporate life of the Church.' The classic example found in the New Testament is of the apostle Peter's mother-in-law, who lay ill when the apostolic band arrived at her house for hospitality. When Jesus healed her, 'she got up at once and began to wait on them' (Luke 4:38).

In the second instance Tim was obeying the biblical instruction to call the 'elders' of the church to pray over him. One of the clergy from St Helen's Bishopsgate, Robert Howarth, joined with the IVF staff for the informal prayer and laying on of hands.

But at the same time he could see nothing 'unspiritual' in also availing himself of the knowledge and experience of the medical profession. Few Christians, in fact, act differently. Most would pray to get better when they are ill, and most would use a sticking plaster and disinfectant when they cut their finger. The problems and disputes arise over the big ailments when medicine – and faith – are stretched to their limits.

For Tim, there was no conflict. 'We have to see that God is so much bigger than we ever thought he was. Everything which exists is his creation; it has a meaning and it matters to God. He has given us the opportunity and responsibility to explore and interact with the world. I thank my consultants and their teams from the depths of my heart because they did something very important. And I thank God that he worked through them: he created them, he gave them gifts. They may not in every case recognise it, but every moment of their existence is being sustained by God.

'People can do good things because they are made in God's image. I went down a certain route and God worked through it. We have a responsibility to make available to ourselves those insights of humanity which are relevant to our condition. To always expect direct healing is to deny that God has made provision for us already. We mustn't act in arrogance and call it faith.'

Despite the fallenness of mankind and the chaos of a suffering world, God is still 'sustaining all things by his powerful word' so that 'in him all things hold together' (Heb. 1:3; Col. 1:17). Or, as the prophet put it:

He who created the heavens and stretched them out,
    who spread out the earth and all that comes out of it,
  (he) gives breath to its people
    and life to those who walk on it (Isa. 42:5).

That means the 'natural' processes of healing – those built into the human body itself and those discovered by medical research – are as much within his control and are part of his purposes as the 'supernatural' interventions which vividly focus his power and bypass or speed up the created systems. It is a human failing rather than a spiritual perception to regard the less spectacular as being also inferior.

That does not give human beings, nor Christians who believe miracles are unlikely to occur today, any reason to put blind faith in the workings of medical science. Prayer for healing is not an optional extra. 'Prayer testifies to our rapport with God; it shows that we identify with God's kingdom and want his rule. It may have an effect which we never see; we should always pray expectantly. I acknowledge the profound importance intercessory prayer has had in my life – but I personally find it very hard to practise. Some people are called to a special ministry of intercession, but none of us can use that as an excuse for not doing it ourselves.'

Tim's experience of healing was a complex affair, not only because of the interwoven strands of medicine and prayer. It also raised the natural question as to why it took so long. If he was a victim of the general imperfection of a fallen world and yet was healed by God, why did he take nearly two years to do it and lead him through the harrowing experiences of drug aversion and depression? What, in other words, was the point of it all?

Occasionally – very occasionally – God's purposes in our experiences become clear. From time to time he most certainly uses the bad things of life to remind us that we are mortal and that we have left undone some of the good things we should have done. 'The wicked prosper and then one day they come face to face with suffering. It says to them, "You thought you were autonomous, that you were master in your own universe" – just like the rich man in Jesus' parable who was filling up his barns. And their suffering makes them think again; it could be good news to them because it turns them to Christ.' C.S. Lewis once wrote that:

> We can rest contentedly in our sins and in our stupidities; and anyone who has watched gluttons shovelling down the most exquisite foods as if they did not know what they were eating, will admit that we can ignore even pleasure. But pain insists on being attended to. God whispers to us in our pleasures, speaks in our conscience, but shouts in our pains; it is His megaphone to rouse a deaf world. [1]

There is no doubt that God is able, and indeed desires, to collect up the evils of the world, even the mistakes and follies of his people, and mould them into his greater and more glorious purposes. That was supremely revealed in the death of Jesus. It was the act of wicked men which could on no account be justified, and yet was transformed into a world-saving event. The devil had done his worst only to discover that he had played straight into God's hands.

It should not be surprising, therefore, that from the timeless perspective of eternity God can take the lesser sufferings of others and weave them into his cosmic tapestry. He said of St Paul, for example, that 'he *must* suffer for my name' (Acts 9:16), and those sufferings included a good number which to any casual observer still seem pointless. St Peter wrote repeatedly of people suffering 'according to God's will' (1 Pet. 3:17, 4:19).

There are lessons in such experiences which, it seems, cannot be learned in any other way. That points to the existence of one possible 'purpose' even if it is not the only or even the main one. The writer to the Hebrews suggests that even Jesus, fully man as well as fully God, needed those lessons in his human experience: 'Although he was a son, he learned obedience from what he suffered' (Heb. 5:8).

The same writer goes on to suggest that if we depend upon God in our experience of suffering we can expect to grow closer to him and become more useful to him later on:

Endure hardship as discipline; God is treating you as sons. For what son is not disciplined by his father? . . . Our fathers disciplined us for a little while as they thought best; but God disciplines us for our good, that we may share in his holiness. No discipline seems pleasant at the time, but painful. Later on, however, it produces a harvest of righteousness and peace for those who have been trained by it (Heb. 12:7, 10, 11).

That does not answer all the questions, of course. But we are dealing with a God who says:

For my thoughts are not your thoughts,
    neither are your ways my ways, declares the Lord,
As the heavens are higher than the earth,
    so are my ways higher than your ways

and my thoughts higher than your thoughts (Isa. 55:8f).

A reason does not have to be known to us in order for it to exist. A purpose does not have to be perceived by us for it to be fulfilled. Faith in the overriding benevolence of God does not depend on our having a sight of his forward planner; it is enough to know that he has one. If we only trust him for as long as he keeps us in comfort and cookies we have not yet emerged from the incipient paganism which regards God (or Nature or Life) as a giant vending machine with an unfortunate habit of getting jammed: 'God's purposes override ours. Therefore healing cannot be automatic, or else God does become just like a chocolate machine.' That provides us with an appropriate context for our prayers for healing.

Prayer 'in the name of Jesus' is primarily an act of worship. It is a declaration of our love for him and a dedication of our wills to his, before it is ever a statement of our longing for some good thing. We want what he wants, because we rest secure in his love. If he withholds some good from us, it is because he has some other, higher good for us to receive. It is arguable, for example, that spiritual virtues are of greater and more lasting value than instant restoration to physical health; and in a fallen world suffering may be one important means for attaining them.

Tim's experience of both suffering and healing convinced him that 'Christianity is not primarily about being happy. There are many enriching things to do with walking with God that may not be comfortable or easy. Life is not about fulfilment, it's about being at peace within oneself and with God – the experience of *shalom*.'

Therefore, in the face of suffering, we pray fervently, trusting in God's undoubted ability and power to do what we ask. We also pray faithfully in the knowledge that we see his purposes only dimly, but that those purposes always issue ultimately in his honour. We do not pray formally, however, going through religious motions and hedging our bets with pious-sounding yet in fact merely shoulder-shrugging phrases such as 'if it is your will', for such come more from faithless resignation rather than obedient submission. And we most emphatically do not pray foolishly, by insisting that God follows our instructions to the letter. God will not listen to the formal or to the foolish, because they do not take him seriously.

When someone is not healed, despite many deeply sincere and believing prayers, we come face to face with the ultimate mysteries of God's plans. Insensitive people can pile on the innuendo about 'lack of faith' on the part of the victim or his praying friends, and burden them with unwarranted feelings of guilt. 'The uniquely Christian response to suffering is not the expectation of healing. I can see so much added pain and suffering in people who get that wrong. I hope he will heal me; I continue to ask him to; my Church will pray that he does. But in the end I am sufficiently confident in what I know of God to accept his judgment.'

We cannot lay the spiritual responsibility for someone's death at the door of the Church in the same way that we can lay the human responsibility for a needless fatality at the feet of the drunken driver. Nor can we credit the devil with a victory in such puzzling circumstances, because that denies God's sovereignty. 'Satan does not have the kind of control that can determine when people die. We can make the devil too big and so deny Christ's power.' Everywhere in the Bible it is God who chooses the time for a person's death, whatever apparent agents he may allow to effect it. Tim had to face the strange fact that some are healed and some are not in his own experience. Why, for example, was he healed, and Janet was not?

Janet was a close friend of Verity, Tim's sister, and he got to know her too. In 1978, she lay dying from cancer. Janet had seen Tim's recovery; she knew that she would not have the same experience.

To those who watched, she suffered unbearably. There came a time when some friends prayed that God would hurry the process of death, to release her from agony. At her funeral the minister referred to a conversation she had had with 'a young man with a potentially terminal illness' (Tim) which she had found helpful, and he quoted her reaction: 'God gave him the right answer, and God has given me the right answer.' Her relatives and friends still found the answer hard to accept. It seemed so pointless.

One day, long after her death, a missionary from South America, home on leave, returned to the British hospital where he had once treated Janet in the early stages of her illness. He gave a talk to the staff Christian Union. Afterwards he learned that three people there had become Christians after observing Janet's life and death. They had been unable to understand how she had kept on smiling as her gentle life faded away.

It was only a fragment of an answer, of course, the merest glimpse of divine purpose, but it helped a bit. It raised almost as many problems as it solved, too. Why could not God have found some less traumatic way of bringing those people to himself? But at least her death was not a total waste. For Tim, though, it was a shattering experience. He attended the funeral, and broke down during the sermon; he was all too aware of his privilege of life, and the pain her death caused others.

And Tim's restored life: was there any discernible purpose in that? No human life committed to the service of Jesus Christ could be anything other than valuable to him, but that again may not be visible to the physical eye. 'God has decided that he wants some people to be with him now, and that's supremely good. He has given them the ultimate healing, they are no longer part of a world in which there is evil and suffering. He has allowed me to live – and that's supremely good too. He made the world good and he means us to enjoy it. God gets much pleasure out of seeing those he created live. But that doesn't make me a great person in his purposes. I might live the next forty years in obscurity.'

Be that as it may, he would live them in the knowledge that his God was close beside him, to comfort and strengthen him, for that above all others was the lesson Tim brought out of the pain, the nausea and the darkness.

'I don't see how anyone could survive what I've had by make-believe. Most people would have said in advance that I wouldn't have been able to stand it. I've been a coward all my life. But when I get into it something gives me a strength and a conviction and a will to fight.

'Pain and despair exist for the Christian; even Paul despaired of life itself. You may feel a hell's distance away from God but he's still there. I had an extraordinarily deep-rooted conviction that I was in God's hands, and that he never left me from one day to the next, even though it was severely threatened by the emotional state I got into.'

Tim is, in fact, the only one of the eleven Hodgkin's patients who received the trial CCNU treatment at the Middlesex to survive. The drug is now used as a second line of attack, and the method of administering it has been drastically altered. The dose is spread over five days, and anyone receiving it today would not experience such violent side-effects.

The conviction of God's presence which had sustained him during that period was, one day, to receive another sore test. But that was after an intermission of ten years which was packed with action. And which was not always trouble-free.

Fourteen

New avenues to explore

Tim threw himself back into his work as arts students travelling secretary with renewed vigour; having learned to drive, he now had greater freedom. He was to continue in the job until the summer of 1976, by which time the IVF had changed its name to UCCF, the Universities and Colleges Christian Fellowship. The three years he spent on the staff became a highpoint in his life, despite the traumas of the treatment. It was an unprecedented time for Bible study, reading, meeting people – and travel.

His wanderlust had official approval. And with his eye for detail, his journeys around Britain became much more than the tourist's check list: done this, seen that. He became fascinated by the varieties of dialect and culture which he encountered, and by the uneven distribution of wealth and poverty. He was not content just to do his job; he wanted to explore and understand the situations he came across.

So, on a visit to Liverpool, he was taken round the notorious Toxteth district to see the appalling housing conditions and the many unemployed people milling about the streets with nothing to do – several years before the area erupted into some of the most violent riots seen up to that time in modern Britain. At the other end of the cultural spectrum he enjoyed conversations with the Scottish colleges traveller Fergus McInlay, himself a former art student. English was only his second language; he read from a Gaelic Bible and wrote Gaelic poetry; he also supported the Scottish Nationalists.

Tim's biggest cultural revelation came when he visited Northern Ireland. Walking down a shopping street, he was startled to see a British soldier across the road pointing a rifle at him, presumably only to focus the sights. He was searched at checkpoints, and watched armoured cars patrolling the streets. He observed the young soldiers, many of them no older – and some younger – than himself, and realised with a shudder that while both he and they were young and British, their lives were at risk in a way his was not, despite his recent illness.

During his first trip to Northern Ireland, someone was shot dead in a nearby street on the first night he was there. One day he drove down the M1 road to Dungannon and passed the spot where, only half an hour later, after a mass breakout from the Maze prison, a prisoner was shot. The troubles seemed to follow him; on his second visit he took the train to Dublin, south of the border, and a bomb went off in the city that night, a fairly rare occurrence. He once borrowed a car and deliberately drove around Belfast's notorious troublespots, strongholds of both Republican and Loyalist extremists, places such as Anderson's Town and the Falls Road. His colleague, an Ulsterman, admitted that he would never have done that, and that Tim had come closer to the violence than he had.

The visits gave him a new awareness of the area's problems, but he did not have to stay in Northern Ireland to solve them. Speaking to one Christian Union, he told them that although he was an outsider, he believed that there was a challenge from the gospel not to ignore the political situation. It was easy for him to point to a Bible text and say that it called them to the task of reconciliation and political justice, but that was its implication in their context; there were different problems to apply it to in England, he said. His belief that the Christian faith was much more than a private relationship with God was already taking on a firmer, broader shape.

Travel was not to be restricted to Britain. While he was still receiving chemotherapy, Tim went with five friends for a holiday in Brittany, on the rugged north-west coast of France. Tony Wales, who was now married, and Meryl Fergus, whose friendship with Malcolm Doney was progressing in that direction and who was then, like Tony, working for the infant Lion Publishing, took Tim and another friend Sue Davies on the camping trip.

Tim was feeling jaded from the treatment, and he had to arrange special travel insurance with an exclusion clause for cancer; he was too big a risk for the actuaries' liking. He was also too weak to share in all the fun; he had to give up the steep climb of Mount St Michel in Normandy and leave the others to complete it. The holiday was another enjoyable exercise in culture spotting. Tony was into cathedral architecture and furnishing, and the group discovered some ornate misericords (carvings in choir stalls) in Rheims Cathedral. Sue, his wife, preferred even older things and took them to see some ancient standing stones at Carnac. Sue Davies was fascinated by the ornately sculptured wayside calvaries depicting Christ's crucifixion. And Tim found wartime bunkers at St Malo, with the marks of ricocheting shells still visible on them.

One evening they went to a restaurant at the French equivalent of England's Land's End. It was quiet, but half of the dining room was laid out in readiness for a party. It turned out to be a wedding reception. It was rowdy and everyone in the restaurant was involved in the toasts. The best man's hilarious impressions of a French singer had Tim in stitches, even though he could not understand the language. As the party warmed up, the guests started racing each other round the room – using chairs as 'horses'.

Tim had also discovered the Netherlands by this time, fallen in love with it, and has visited it many times since. It suited his typically English preference for a place which is a bit like home; the majority of people speak English, radios can pick up English broadcasts and even some English TV programmes are networked. Yet it was sufficiently different to satisfy his curiosity. The landscape in particular had intrigued him: the vast expanses of flat emptiness with no bushes, only occasional rows of poplars breaking the scene; the fields being divided by ditches. The elevated waterways can create an almost surreal experience, as the traveller notices a boat above him as he drives along a road, or a field of cows below him as he sails on a lake.

Having got to know Graham Birtwistle, the English art history lecturer working with Professor Rookmaaker in Amsterdam, Tim had a natural contact who could introduce him to the country and provide a base for exploring it. He made other Dutch friends too and, not surprisingly, they appear on stage at significant points in the later scenes of his story.

But there was to be a deep sadness mingled with the joy of discovering Holland. The man who had first introduced Tim to the country – before he had ever visited it – through his lectures on seventeenth century Dutch paintings, Professor Hans Rookmaaker, died unexpectedly in 1977. For the circle of friends, that event became a watershed, rather like the death of American President John F. Kennedy; they could remember vividly what they were doing at the time. Tim was out until very late. When he arrived home there was a note from Malcolm and Meryl Doney waiting for him. It told him to go to their house (which was ten minutes away) whatever time of night it happened to be; it was urgent. When he arrived, about midnight, they told him that Rookmaaker had suffered a fatal heart attack; he was not yet sixty years of age.

By that time Tim was a student again. The desire to work in the film world still burned inside him, and when he left UCCF in the summer of 1976 he felt he needed to re-educate himself on the subject. Previously, he had taken two years practical training at the London Film School; now he wanted to broaden his theoretical knowledge. He enrolled for a two year post-graduate course in the Film Studies Department of the Slade School of Fine Art, at University College, London. Unfortunately, he had no money to pay for his tuition or living expenses; the UCCF salary had been adequate but he had not been able to save much from it. And he failed to get a government grant.

He was convinced that the Slade was God's place for him for the next couple of years, so he thought about sponsorship. Why not ask his wide circle of acquaintances to contribute £1 a month for two years? He needed about £1200 a year, so 100 people could support him with little sacrifice on their part. His friends Brian Griffiths (the economics and banking lecturer, and later government advisor) and Tony Wales put their signatures to a circular letter appealing for support. The promises came in; the money was raised.

Meanwhile the college continued applying on his behalf for a bursary. Four times Tim's name had gone forward as a deserving candidate, and four times the application was rejected. The authorities tried once more: and succeeded. Tim returned the money he had received from friends.

The Slade Film Studies Department was dominated by a majority of Marxist students; Tim, as a Christian, was something of a Daniel in a den of lions, and the lions were not always very friendly towards his views. In one incident, the students held a sit-in to protest about financial cuts in education, and especially in grants to students from overseas. Tim was also opposed to the government policy, but he was equally opposed to the methods of protest employed by the students – a stance which baffled them. Unwittingly, he became the articulate voice of opposition to their tactics. As the tension in the college grew, he persuaded the college bursar not to call in the police to break up the demonstration, and then he tabled a motion to end the strike. He was likely to win the vote, so the organisers put up their own motion, couched in emotive political rhetoric. It had the same effect; normal college life resumed, and a potentially violent confrontation was avoided.

For the last six months of his course he buried himself in writing a thesis on *Cinema Verité*, the 'fly on the wall' technique of making documentary films by following people with a camera, and letting their actions and words speak for themselves without additional narration. This was his first experience of writing a major work, and one of the college lecturers corrected his style and introduced him to such literary snares as split infinitives, an exercise used to helpfully prepare him for the time when he would become a magazine editor.

From the rarified heights of the Slade, where he watched over 200 films, he descended in 1978 to the basement of Scripture Union's London bookshop in Wigmore Street, where he helped to build a darkroom. He was back at the odd jobs, and SU proved yet again to be a faithful backstop. Sue Davies, the sixth member of the Brittany holiday party, was working at the BBC; one day Tim met her and asked her to let him know if any jobs were going at Broadcasting House. Within half an hour she phoned him: the Radio 1 programme *Mailbag* needed a freelance researcher. He applied, and in January 1979 launched into three years' varied experience as a researcher and producer in radio and TV.

He began by working half a week on *Mailbag*, but in less than two months was asked to work the rest of the week on another programme, *Stayin' Alive*. He took to radio much as a duck takes to water; he enjoyed the medium and found he had a natural feel for it.

Without pushing his Christian views in an aggressive manner, he proposed and then compiled a *Mailbag* special on 'Is Christianity Eyewash?' He also suggested to Radio 1 that the Greenbelt Arts Festival, an annual event held over the late August bank holiday weekend, was worthy of their attention. Sited in Bedfordshire, it was then attracting about 10,000 young people, and has expanded considerably since. The idea was accepted, and Tim arranged the first ever national programme devoted solely to Greenbelt. It featured an exclusive preview of Cliff Richard's latest album *Rock 'n' Roll Juvenile* which included the hit singles 'We don't talk any more' and 'Carrie'. Cliff had invariably refused requests for exclusive previews in the past. Since that time, Greenbelt has been covered by either Radio 1 or

BBC TV most years.

Tim later researched and presented features on Radio 4 *Woman's Hour*; one was about alternative therapies for cancer, another was a 'detective story' about an ancient can of nitrate film (which is highly flammable and has the same chemical base as gunpowder) found by David Porter, and which Tim investigated to discover if it was valuable. (It was not.) On another occasion he brought his film interests into radio with a documentary for the arts programme *Kaleidoscope* about the National Film Archive; it proved to certain sceptics within radio that an audio programme about a visual library was not only possible but also entertaining and informative.

For nine months during 1981 and early 1982 he worked full-time for Lella Productions on the *Jesus Then and Now* video series, and appeared in several of the programmes. It featured Canon David Watson, who later died of cancer, and produced the usual crop of film-makers' headaches. On one occasion the crew was filming a sequence about Jesus as the 'lamb of God', with David Watson speaking to camera in a field of sheep in Wales. It was pouring with rain (which does not show up on video or film unless it is lit from behind or is falling against a dark background) and Tim and the team had to devise ways of keeping David Watson looking dry and fresh, and to prevent his script from becoming soggy.

During that period one of Tim's spare time activities was to serve on the editorial advisory board of the Christian magazine *Third Way*. Started in 1977 by the publishers of *Crusade* (which later became *Today*), it aimed to provide a thoughtful and biblical perspective to social, political, moral and cultural issues. It was one of the products of the 1970s' emergence of evangelical Christians from an exclusive concern for private piety towards a biblical critique of society.

The *Third Way* editor's chair fell vacant in 1981 and several of his friends urged Tim to consider taking it over. He was reluctant at first, largely because of his vested interest; he was involved in producing a review of its policy as a basis for future development. He did not want to be handed a job on a plate, only for the publishers to subsequently find he was not the most suitable candidate. He agreed to apply when they publicly advertised the post and was interviewed, along with five others who had been shortlisted. He had been up for several interviews for jobs within broadcasting, and was getting tired of always coming second; he also felt that, because he was well-known to the interviewers, we would not give him a fair deal. Convinced he would be failed again, he almost failed himself by allowing his aggression to boil over in the interview. But to his own surprise he was offered the job, which he still holds at the time of writing.[1]

That incident was not the only point when he made a bad error of judgment. God, he reckoned, had given him his life back after Hodgkin's Disease, but God had not turned him into a machine. He still retained his human freedom, and he was as free to make a mess of his life as he was free to use it in God's service. Perhaps still suffering from the long-term emotional effects of the illness and treatment of the mid-1970s, he pursued one close personal relationship with more haste than wisdom. It was an unmitigated disaster and sent ripples of hurt and anxiety across Tim's wide pool of acquaintances. The waters remained muddied for some time.

In looking for happiness, he had found pain and rejection; maybe he looked too hard and grasped too quickly. Chastened and shaken, he recovered to view the experience as one more hard knock along the hazard-strewn way of Christian discipleship. Time would erase the worst of the memories, and the assurance of divine forgiveness sincerely sought and received would remove the whole of the guilt. The experience underlined a lesson he had been slow to learn, but which, from then on, was to become increasingly evident in his life; the action man had to become a better listener and a wiser judge; and he did.

The ten years from 1975 to 1985 saw as much change in

the world as in Tim's own life. Politicians came and went; Jimmy Carter gave way to Ronald Reagan in the USA; the Tory Margaret Thatcher took over from Labour's James Callaghan as British Prime Minister; Mrs Gandhi fell from grace and rose again to power in India; and the Shah left Iran. War broke out between Iran and Iraq and between Israel and Lebanon in the Middle East, ceased in Vietnam and sparked briefly in the Falkland Islands, where British forces went into action against the Argentinians. There were three Popes in Italy and three Archbishops in England; one black bishop became the first Prime Minister of the new independent state of Zimbabwe, and another was murdered by Idi Amin's forces of terror in Uganda.

There were riots in Brixton, Toxteth and Moss Side which led to the Scarman Report; a peace agreement between Israel and Egypt was reached at Camp David in the USA, and the SALT II arms talks were signed by the USSR and the USA – but the world still seethed with unrest.

Unemployment rose from less than one million to over three million in Britain, which had joined the European Economic Community, begun to export North Sea oil, and seen the establishment of the Social Democratic Party. The Brandt Report on the third world was debated but not acted upon by the governments of the developed countries, which left it to a British TV news reporter to alert the public to horrendous famine in Ethiopia and to an Irish pop singer to raise massive 'Live Aid' cash gifts for it.

Also swept along by the swirling currents of change were Tim's friends. Tony Wales became a director of Lion Publishing, which had grown considerably over the years. Meryl Doney had left Lion and given birth to two children, writing and editing children's books while her husband Malcolm became assistant editor of *Today* magazine, before turning freelance author and copywriter. Norman Stone became a successful documentary and drama director for BBC TV; among his credits was the BAFTA award-winning dramatisation of the life of C. S. Lewis and his love for his cancer-stricken wife Joy. Along the way

Norman married TV presenter Sally Magnusson, daughter of *Mastermind* quiz master Magnus Magnusson. David Porter worked with Scripture Union Publishing before becoming a freelance writer and editor.

Perhaps the biggest change of all for Tim came in 1981. With his hair and beard now a little shorter and neater, and his figure slightly filled out, he married Margaret Garner, a music and religious education teacher in Guildford. She had joined the UCCF staff in September 1976, just after Tim had left, but recalls noticing him at a staff conference the previous July as someone who looked quite out of place in what she considered the UCCF to be.

In common with other UCCF personnel, she used his convenient London apartment for occasional committee meetings. By then Tim was living in Linden Mansions, a plain block of flats near Archway in north London which had been home, it seemed, to generations of students and travelling secretaries. Meryl Fergus had lived there long before she became Meryl Doney, and it was there that her future husband Malcolm had retreated to on the night the ceiling in Highbury Park fell where his head might have been.

The couple only began to get to know each other closely after Margaret left UCCF and returned to her former teaching job. Their relationship did not have the most auspicious start. They went to the cinema together. Margaret realised that Tim would want to discuss the film, Bunuel's *That Obscure Object of Desire*, so she concentrated hard. Tim began the discussion as predicted, then he realised that she had entirely missed the point of the film: two separate actresses had shared the leading lady's role.

He did not seem to mind. The joke was on him when he took Margaret to a Chinese restaurant. He ordered the meal, and then fell asleep. Margaret at first feared that he was bored with her company, but he was just tired. The smell of the food revived him.

The thought that she was marrying someone who had had cancer did not affect her greatly. Tim had stopped taking his daily maintaining drug, and the possibility that his original cancer could recur had all but vanished even by their wedding day. Margaret had married a healthy man who once, before she had ever known him, had been dangerously ill. He was not a man who was clinging desperately to life by his finger tips. Their relationship had never been cloyed by nagging doubts or fears for the future; Murphy's Law ('whatever can go wrong, will') was neither written in their Bible nor formulated in their creed.

But she did receive a shock when she discovered something about his treatment which even he had been unaware of. The chemotherapy had rendered him sterile.

By one of those accidents of miscommunication, the possibility had never reached his ears. As soon as he heard about it, after he had been going out with Margaret for a while, he had the necessary tests and they confirmed his worst fears: he could never be a father. He was as distraught for Margaret as for himself; he was fearful that the oversight could have given her false hopes and expectations.

It was certainly a harsh blow; she loved children. But she loved Tim more. There was no way, she decided, that she could, or would wish to, refuse to marry him just because she could not have children by him. It was something they would have to learn to live through together.

She was cushioned to an extent by the fact that she had often had to go without things which other people accepted as normal. She was the daughter of an Anglican clergyman in Weymouth, a port on the south coast of England. The family, like most clerical families, had not been able to afford the adventurous holidays other children at her school had been able to go on; she had never had a large wardrobe of clothes to show off. As she had grown up, she had never assumed even that she would necessarily marry, and as she moved into her late twenties the possibility had seemed more remote until she met Tim.

Margaret accepted the fact that she could not have Tim's children, a little bemused as to why God should deal her such a blow, but not embittered towards him. As for any single person or childless couple, Mother's Day services and other family occasions in the church calendar inevitably placed an added emotional strain on her, reminding her of joys she could never fully know.

The wedding went ahead; the couple settled into their semi-detached house in Guildford close to the main railway line. Both had steady and rewarding jobs and they made good friends in their local Anglican church (Emmanuel, Stoughton). They began to think of adopting; the idea of a multi-racial family especially appealed to them. Margaret's family had links with Africa, Tim's with the Far East, so they were no strangers to the wider world. And as non-white children are often the hardest to place with adoptive parents, it also seemed a potentially small but meaningful practical contribution to a human problem.

Then their world was shaken to its foundations by a totally unexpected piece of news, and their horizons suddenly contracted. As Tim was to write in *Third Way* twelve months later, 'Looking back on 1985, it appears that much that was on the public agenda wasn't on mine . . . In Rip van Winkle style, it was as if I had slept through it all. (Come to think of it, I probably did.)'[2]

His hibernation began after a remarkable series of events.

Fifteen

In the nick of time

We met in the dim, cavernous foyer of the Middlesex Hospital, its walls bedecked with paintings and a roll of honour, giving it more of the atmosphere of an ancient university than of a modern, bustling teaching hospital. Only the flower stall opposite the porters' desk, and the rows of wooden chairs for waiting visitors, challenged that initial impression, until a nurse or two in uniform hurried through the foyer from one wing of the building to the other. Not a whiff of disinfectant tickled the nose. Outside, the winter air was warmer than the seasonal average; inside, the hospital was almost summery.

Tim Dean was the only occupant of the chairs. We exchanged greetings and then turned left towards the Oncology Department in the west wing. It was late morning on Thursday 10 January 1985, the day of his annual check-up. It was almost exactly a decade after the nightmare of Hodgkin's Disease had faded into the dawn of new hope and renewed life.

This book was already in the making; the publishers had asked us to write about the Hodgkin's period. We had arranged that Dr Gillian Vaughan Hudson should give us a guided tour of the wards where he had been treated, to refresh his memory and provide fine detail for the narrative. She had been his Registrar (senior physician) during the second occurrence of Hodgkin's Disease, and continued to be the doctor who saw him for his check-ups. In the years since Tim's illness, she had become the Deputy Director of the British National Lymphoma Investigation, and Honorary Senior Registrar at the Middlesex.

We found her in a small office. Despite the high ceilings and seemingly endless corridors, the treatment area felt cramped and cluttered. By contrast, the wards were bright and spacious; they had been altered and decorated since Tim's day.

There was a conference of nurses in Greenhow Ward; Gillian Vaughan Hudson interrupted it to introduce Tim as 'someone who was with us some years ago with Advanced Hodgkin's.' Surprise registered on several of the young women's faces. They knew that only about a quarter of such patients lived to tell the tale. Behind them, lying in rows of beds, were mostly ageing and very sick men. Before them stood a tall, lean young man in his mid-thirties, who strode purposefully down the ward, sporting a tidy beard and wearing a neat shirt, tie and jacket. On the wards, the nurses generally saw only the most difficult Hodgkin's cases; the more responsive ones were now mainly treated as outpatients – a big advance in the chemotherapy process had taken place since 1975.

The time for Tim's appointment was drawing close. He asked if he could be late, so that we could have a quick lunch together first. Gillian agreed; 'Come when you're ready,' she said. 'We'll still be here!' Things at the Middlesex were still as flexible as they had been all those years before. Nevertheless, they were no less vigilant.

Tim's routine blood sample passed through the usual laboratory examination; the white cells were counted. White blood cells are the body's own healing agents. About seventy-five per cent of them are called 'phagocytes' and are formed in the bone marrow, and almost all of them are 'neutrophils'. They eat up living germs, remove dirt or damaged body tissue, and surround infected or wounded areas. A small proportion of phagocytes are called 'monocytes'. The remaining twenty-five per cent of white cells are the 'lymphocytes' formed in the lymph nodes, and produce anti-bodies and anti-toxins in the fight against disease.

His overall white cell count was within normal limits.

The monocyte count was also within normal limits, but a little high. And then the haematologist noticed an odd-looking white cell. There was nothing actually wrong with it; but it did not look right, either. 'Iffy,' she called it.

The next day she drew it to the attention of the Consultant, David Linch. When they looked for it again under the microscope, they could not find it; it was, after all, only one in many thousands. But instinct is stronger than reason, and the doctors became cautious. There was just a chance – statistically very small – that another cancer related to the punishing drug treatment Tim had received a decade before could have developed. Medical experience, however, indicated that he should have got it much sooner after Hodgkin's Disease, if he was to get it at all.

So it was on the basis of a corporate hunch that something might be wrong, yet with only a slightly high white cell count and an odd looking cell which they could no longer find as their only evidence, contrasted with the fact that Tim had an otherwise clean bill of health, that the doctors decided to call him back for more tests. They were very casual about it, and asked him to arrange another appointment.

On Thursday 7 February, he presented himself at the Consultant's office. David Linch explained that the slightly high monocyte count could have been caused by any number of factors, from glandular fever to a viral infection. The cells multiply in order to surround and destroy alien agents in the blood stream. He wanted to take another blood sample and screen it carefully to find the cause of the high count.

'There's also the extremely rare possibility that the drugs you had may have damaged your bone marrow,' he added. 'So we'd like to test that too.'

Tim suddenly felt very flat. He sighed. He was in the middle of a very busy period. Editing the monthly magazine *Third Way* with only one part-time editorial assistant was an exhausting and time-consuming job in itself. In addition, he was also giving a series of lectures at Trinity College Bristol, where most of the 130 students were training for the Anglican ministry. He was teaching part of the media studies course, on TV communications. And after ten years of good health, 'I hoped I'd got to the end of being fiddled about with by hospitals.'

The doctors knew their patient well. They remembered that he had taken a close interest in the details of his previous illness and treatment, so they assumed that he would know the real reason why they wanted to take a bone marrow test. In fact, he did not; the thought that he might have cancer again did not cross his mind. They had prepared a contingency plan in case he reacted badly to the idea of the test; they would forget it but call him back in three months' time for another blood test.

The interview was relaxed. There was no sense of urgency. David Linch gently pressed Tim for an answer. Discretion triumphed over desire; he agreed that if they wanted to do the test, then they should.

The doctor who took the samples had two different bone marrow tests available to her. She could do the 'aspirate' test which drew off some bone marrow fluid. Or she could do the more difficult 'trephine' test which removed a small piece of bone tissue. David Linch had intended that only the aspirate should be done, but she did not know that and so did both. She took the samples, and some more blood, and Tim was to report back to the hospital a week later, when he was due for a routine heart test, done at his own request because of a higher than average incidence of angina in his family.

There was nothing wrong with his blood; there were no viruses to be found in it, and certainly no malignant nor even odd-looking cells. The results of the aspirate test were also good; the fluid was quite normal. There were some sighs of relief, but they would still call Tim back for a further blood test in three months, just to be safe.

Twenty-four hours later came the result of the trephine test, which David Linch had not requested. The sample was jammed with cancerous cells.

When Tim returned to the hospital on Thursday 14

February – St Valentine's Day – he was sent in to see Gillian Vaughan Hudson and David Linch. He handed them the results of the heart test; he had no problems there. They put it to one side.

David Linch got straight to the point. 'Tim, I'm afraid that the news is not good,' he said. 'You've got leukaemia. I want you in hospital tomorrow.'

Tim was stunned; the strength drained from him. Tears welled up in his eyes, and a few escaped. But his first thoughts were not of self-pity. 'How on earth do I tell Margaret and my parents?' he asked.

David Linch offered to break the news himself, but that had not been Tim's concern. How to do it was not the issue; the effect it would have on them was. He knew what he would have to go through. The thought of Margaret, his bride of three and a half years, having to watch him pass through that hell was overwhelming. And his parents, it seemed, had had more than their fair share of anxiety about their offspring. Quite apart from Tim's previous cancer, his brother Tony had almost died of glandular fever when he was twenty-one, and his sister Verity was still sometimes troubled by a long-standing and crippling psychiatric illness. How much more could they take? 'To know in a split second the pain that you're going to introduce into other people's lives – that really shook me up.'

Third Way was at a critical point in its production cycle. The March issue was due to go to press the following week; it would collapse if he just walked out on it now. He needed time. 'Rule number one in the National Health Service is negotiate with the doctors. If there's an absolute they'll never be swayed, but in some areas you can negotiate. So I said, "Do you really need me in tomorrow? Can I come in on Monday? I need a day to sort out my affairs at work." '

Monday, he was told, would be soon enough. But there was no other alternative. The treatment would last for at least six weeks, some of which he would have to spend in isolation. The chemotherapy would send his neutrophil count so low that he could die if he caught a minor infection; his body would temporarily lose most of its natural defences.

He asked what his chances of survival were; he knew that leukaemia was potentially more lethal than Hodgkin's Disease. 'We are hopeful,' was the laconic reply. No promises, and no time limits; just hope.

And even that was pretty thin. His body had taken such a thrashing from the previous treatment that private medical opinion, not yet passed on to Tim, reckoned that there was little likelihood that he could survive for long with leukaemia. The disease, it later transpired, was directly related to the Hodgkin's treatment; just under one per cent of Hodgkin's patients in the UK had also developed leukaemia.

There are several different forms of leukaemia, some more potentially lethal than others. Many chronic leukaemias are containable – even curable – and patients can lead a reasonable life for many years. But Tim had acute myeloid leukaemia, which spreads rapidly and can be fatal within weeks unless it is treated quickly. It is caused by a cancerous change in the neutrophils. The cells multiply rapidly, disrupting the production of red blood cells and platelets (orange-coloured blood clotting agents), and they invade the bloodstream and vital organs.

It is a rare disease, and the treatment does not always effect a cure. Tim's case, being secondary to Hodgkin's was extremely rare; only a handful of people were known by the British National Lymphoma Register to have had it – and the majority had died. Had he developed it a dozen years previously, at the time of his Hodgkin's Disease, he probably would have been dead within three months. But medical knowledge had progressed; the doctors knew how it might be cured. And it had been caught in the very earliest stage, by the remarkable coincidence of a routine annual check, an alert haematologist, and a doctor who did two bone marrow tests instead of one.

The interview was over. As they parted, Tim asked Gillian Vaughan Hudson to visit him in the hospital as a friend. Leukaemia patients were managed by the haematology (blood) department rather than her oncology (cancer) department, so she would not be his Registrar this time. She readily agreed.

He had planned to attend a lecture that evening at Gresham College in the Barbican Centre. He would have to miss it; there were too many other pressing things to do now. But he was not yet ready to go home, nor back to the office. He needed a friend to talk to first.

Still shaken, and aware that the future was again a vacuum of uncertainty, he went to a telephone in the Outpatients Department and dialled a local number. It belonged to David Winter, head of religious broadcasting for BBC Radio, whose office was a few minutes walk away. Tim asked to see him; he said only that he had some bad news.

The two men had known each other for some time. Tim had worked within the BBC, of course, and both had also been closely involved with the Arts Centre Group since its earliest days. David Winter had been chairman of it for a while; its ministry to professional artists and media personnel had grown, and it had moved from the Kensington premises where the early students' Bible studies were held, to property linked to a church near the Old Vic theatre in Waterloo. He had someone with him when Tim phoned, but within fifteen minutes the two men were drinking coffee together. Within an hour they were laughing together, too, their conversation having wandered far from the subject of leukaemia. Tim was relaxing, recovering, even, from the blow, and beginning to put together a strategy for the next three days before his world would suddenly shrink to the confines of a small hospital room, and the fight to save his life would begin.

David Winter at once shed some light onto the gloom. He talked of a member of his staff with cancer who had been given three weeks to live – and who was still alive two years later. (He has since died). A doctor in his church had told him how leukaemia patients were no longer given any estimate of life expectancy, because the odds were getting better all the time.

Tim got a similar message when he arrived back at his office later in the afternoon. Since he had become editor of *Third Way* the Thirty Press, which had begun the magazine in 1977 as a companion to *Today* (formerly *Crusade*), had merged with the publishers of two other magazines, *Buzz* and *Family*. (The company is now called Elm House Christian Communications.) One result of the merger had been an office move from central London (sub-let from the Scripture Union City Road headquarters) to New Malden, a mainly residential suburb between Wimbledon and Kingston, a few miles south-west.

He had phoned his managing director, Brian Phillips, from David Winter's office, told him the news, and said he was coming back to the office to talk over the implications. Brian happened to know of someone who had been cured of leukaemia. Tim was quickly getting the message that there really was hope. He called up Veronica Zundel, his part-time assistant editor, and asked her to come in the next day. He also phoned his brother and sister and broke the news to them.

Then he drove home to Guildford to tell Margaret. She was already there after a day teaching, but she had not stopped working. She also gave private after-school piano lessons to children who came to the house, and she was in the middle of one when Tim arrived home early; she was not expecting him until late.

He went into the kitchen, brewed himself some tea, and waited. Margaret came in when the lesson was finished and the pupil safely dispatched home. As their eyes met, Tim rehearsed the simple line: 'I've got leukaemia.' They fell into each other's arms, and wept. There was nothing else they could do.

They decided to tell Tim's parents face to face, so that evening they drove the few miles to the bungalow in Virginia Water. It was in darkness. Tim left Margaret in the car and went to the door. There was no reply when he rang the bell. He waited, and rang again. There were no noises inside, no lights on. As he turned to walk away, Margaret called from the car; she had seen a light.

Eventually, Tim's mother Joan opened the door. It was not late, but she was already in her night clothes. Both she and her husband Len had been in bed all day, suffering from a heavy bout of flu. They were in no state to receive bad news, but they had to be told. Naturally, they were distraught. Tim could not expose himself unnecessarily to infection, so he could not risk staying to comfort them and to give them time to come to terms with the facts. They prayed together, then Tim and Margaret hurried out of the bungalow. It was the worst possible start to the weekend.

The next day, Friday, he had to tell the office staff at New Malden. He wanted no whisper campaign which could easily give rise to rumour or awkward embarrassment. The whole staff of Elm House, about thirty people involved in the production and dispatch of the four magazines, were asked to down tools and assemble for a special meeting. Brian Phillips handed it over to Tim.

'You're gathered together on my account,' he said. 'Some of you know that twelve years ago I had cancer, although I've been fine since. Yesterday I was diagnosed as having leukaemia. On Monday I go into hospital for about six weeks. I would be grateful for your prayers for Margaret and myself.'

Such directness characterised the rest of the weekend. There was no point in being any different; the facts would not change, and no amount of verbal padding would soften their impact. He had one thing on his side; he had passed this way before. He knew that open talk was a direct route to inner acceptance, for himself and for others. Second-hand medical stories are about as reliable as a weather forecast based on seaweed. No one would be helped by the inevitable exaggeration, uncertainty or misconceptions.

Besides, it was nothing to be ashamed of; it was no ugly skeleton to be locked safely away, no nasty dirt to be brushed quickly beneath the carpet, to be hidden from the neighbours. Illness was not a personal failure; it was an accident of life, like a bad back or a broken leg – only in this case rather worse. Not that it was easy to talk about, or to bear. The artwork for the March issue of *Third Way* was more than once dampened by the tears of both Tim and Veronica Zundel, as they raced to get it ready for the printer.

Back home, Tim began a telephone marathon which lasted through the weekend. He contacted a long list of friends and gave them the same simple message: 'I've got leukaemia . . .' Three-quarters of the weekend, it seemed, was spent on the telephone, and the other quarter in tears. But on Saturday evening they went for a meal with his sister Verity and her husband Mervyn. It could have been a sober affair broken by false joviality. They did laugh a lot, in fact; Verity's two children (born since Tim's Hodgkin's treatment) helped matters considerably by finding it incomprehensible that Uncle Tim could be so seriously ill, yet at the same time be the life and soul of the party.

He had taken the initiative. Planting himself in a large armchair he explained that, 'This time it could be curtains for me. If that is what God is going to do, then that's right and I'll accept it. But cancer is an evil, and I mean to fight it.' It was to be a recurring theme in the coming months, and with good reason. The fight was intense.

In the twelve days between the trephine bone marrow test and his admission into hospital, the leukaemia had spread to his blood. There was no time to lose.

And once in hospital, he again became a shadow of his former self.

Sixteen

Solitary confinement

Tim began almost where he had left off. He was back on Greenhow Ward, and a side room had been held for him; he would need it when he went into isolation. It was providentially large as far as single hospital rooms go, a bay window looking down onto the uninspiring back offices of Independent Television News adding to the floor area. It had two easy chairs, a TV, and the standard bedside locker.

Verity drove Tim and Margaret into London on Monday 18 February, and soon both women had an early introduction to Tim's approach to hospital life. He spent part of the day finding out the nurses' Christian names. One nurse poked her head round the door and enquired rather nervously if she could ask him some questions and fill out the standard forms. She needed to do it privately; among the potentially difficult or embarrassing questions was: 'Do you know why you have come into hospital?' Margaret suddenly began to feel her age; the house doctor looked like one of her sixth form pupils. Gillian Vaughan Hudson came in to explain what would be happening in the treatment, and to meet Margaret.

On Tuesday Tim had a minor operation under general anaesthetic to insert a Hickman Line. A tube was fitted into his chest so that drugs and transfusions could be fed directly into a main artery near his heart. It avoided the need for frequent injections and skin punctures; blood samples could also be taken from it.

And on Wednesday his temperature soared to 103°F (39.4°C) and his spirits sank. It was like going back to the

Hodgkin's sweats, only this time he had an infection probably – and annoyingly – picked up during the operation. He sucked ice cubes and had an electric fan to cool him. The chemotherapy began the same day.

'It was the unreal situation again. I felt OK before I went into hospital, and I was told that I'd got something in me which I couldn't see or feel but which was killing me. Then they gave me an operation through which I got an infection, and they smashed me with chemotherapy. It's bizarre. If only when you had acute cancer you got pain to tell you.' All he had experienced in the way of symptoms was a slight tiredness (but he had been working hard), aching bones and a slightly clouded feeling in his head. They were in effect flu symptoms and no doctor nor hypochondriac on earth could have associated that common complaint with an extremely rare cancer.

Once again the drugs were very powerful. They usually made him sick, although the reaction was not nearly so violent as it had been with the CCNU he had received for Hodgkin's Disease. In order to reduce the side-effects, he was given a pre-med (a strong sedative usually administered before the general anaesthetic in a surgical operation). This reduced him to a semi-conscious state for hours at a time.

In his sleep, he muttered and moaned. When he was awake, his voice became croaky and he could only talk slowly, a few muttered words at a time. When visitors came – Margaret included – he had no desire or energy for conversation. When he managed to stagger round the room, it looked as though he had been placed in a time machine and shot into the future, to become a frail, almost senile, old man. It was a dramatic drug-induced personality change.

There were other changes, too. His hair and beard started to fall out as if in protest, refusing to co-exist with the strange, obnoxious toxins flowing into his body. It is a common side-effect of chemotherapy, although his Hodgkin's treatment had not made him so completely bald as did the leukaemia treatment. He also lost weight, and discovered that another familiar reaction had made an unwelcome return: he had difficulty in swallowing pills. He had overcome his old aversion in the intervening years, being quite able to take aspirin when he needed it, but in hospital he found swallowing was not so easy.

What was new – and harmless – was the occasionally peculiar effect of the drugs on his behaviour. On Thursday night he went to bed wearing green pyjamas. He woke up the next morning with a green top and red bottoms; the green trousers were neatly folded in his locker. He had apparently been delirious and changed them in his sleep during the night, for no reason. In the middle of another night a nurse found him looking for a pair of socks, which he did not need.

And then there was the isolation. Solitary confinement is generally regarded as the worst form of imprisonment; it increases the psychological pressure on a person and when it is combined with sleep deprivation or physical torture it can speed up a stubborn prisoner's breakdown and 'confession'.

After the drugs had done their destructive work on his white blood cells, cancerous and healthy alike, Tim was defenceless against bacterial or viral attack. He was languishing in the Dark Ages, when the common cold could kill. His only hope for survival was to stay cocooned in his sterile cell. And the doctors said that a percentage of patients who lived in such conditions had broken down into screaming fits, pleading to be let out. They did remember one person who had so enjoyed his hermitage that he feigned sleep when visitors arrived, but he was an exception. Tim, ever gregarious, was not likely to find much pleasure in extended isolation in a small room.

On Wednesday 27 February 1985 the barrier came down for the first time on his twelve-foot square side ward with beige walls and a back-street window. The house of healing had become a prison of loneliness and monotony. Anyone who entered it had to don a plastic apron, face mask and

gloves (having washed their hands first), before opening
the door.

Man was not made to be alone. Nor to be incarcerated in
a cramped space. Especially when he knew that the cell
could become a tomb. But the sociable thirty-four year old
had devised a strategy for maintaining his sanity. His
attention to detail and flair for organisation came to his
rescue.

Even prisoners are .normally allowed outside visitors.
Tim was granted three – and they would be barred if they
had the slightest snuffle. On no account could they touch
him. He chose them carefully.

First, obviously and naturally, was Margaret, his wife.
He could not envisage surviving without seeing her each
day, and in the event her presence became crucial to his
morale. Miraculously she never once caught a cold while he
was in isolation; she was normally vulnerable to the coughs
and sneezes of school children and staff colleagues. Tim
had only been in hospital a couple of days when she
travelled home on the train, rather than by car. The train
was packed and she was stuck next to a woman who had a
cold. Later in the saga she was driven to London by a friend
who went down with flu the next day. She prayed for
protection, and clearly received it.

The second regular visitor was his brother Tony, who
lived and worked an hour's drive north-west of London.
When Tim had broken the news about leukaemia, Tony
had promised to give whatever help was asked for. As he
was the only blood relative likely to be able to make
frequent, almost daily, visits, and as the two men had
grown closer over the past decade, Tim asked him to visit,
and Tony gladly agreed.

The third was a relatively new friend, Steve Nickless,
who worked nearby in the university health service as a
doctor. He could call in on his way home from work each
day. Steve was someone Tim could talk to about a wide
range of contemporary issues, thus keeping his mind alert
and off his own condition; and Steve's knowledge of the

medical processes gave him added value as a sympathetic listener and counsellor.

Then Tim exercised his habit of negotiation; he asked if he could have a fourth visitor. It was not a particularly selfish or cheeky request; he wanted his own personal chaplain, for good reasons.

He took a certain amount of delight in throwing the hospital categorising system into disarray by putting 'Christian' on the admission form in the space left for 'religion'. It almost guaranteed that he would not see the official hospital chaplains who visited patients according to their Church denomination. During his Hodgkin's Disease period it was a long time before any chaplain came; in the end the non-conformist chaplain came and explained that 'Christian' could only mean non-Anglican or non-Roman Catholic. During the leukaemia treatment he was visited first by the honorary free church chaplain, Dr John Newton, then also minister of the West London (Methodist) Mission, who proved to be a regular and stimulating visitor, and then later by the Anglicans.

Even though he knew he could have asked for regular visits from the official chaplains (who like the other hospital staff were permitted into his room when necessary), he wanted someone he knew in advance that he could relate to spiritually, and who would also have the special added responsibility of seeing him through the dark days which he knew were coming; perhaps, even, of seeing him through the door of death itself.

His request was granted, and he chose Roger Simpson, a former contemporary on the UCCF staff and then one of the curates at All Souls Langham Place, close by the Middlesex Hospital. Roger's prime task was to read the Bible and pray with Tim regularly, whether the patient felt like it or not. They frequently had holy communion together, bending the rules somewhat because Roger, as the celebrant dressed in the unclerical garb of apron, gloves and mask, could not take the bread and wine himself in the room. But neither that, nor the fact that he occasionally

forgot to bring the bread and made do with cream crackers
scrounged from the ward kitchen, lessened the efficacy of
the sacrament to its recipient. Those times helped to keep
Tim on the emotional and spiritual rails. They used the
Anglican service book, the set responses giving Tim an
opportunity to join in without having to struggle for words
when his emotions felt flat or his mind was dazed by drugs.

Roger was the only one of his visitors who was normally
able to see him in the daytime; the others were all restricted
to evenings and weekends by their jobs. So that left the
long days to fill. Tim devised a routine to stave off the
potential boredom for the times when he felt well and
energetic, because the adverse effects of the chemotherapy
had worn off.

He found the hospital regime of early to sleep, early to
rise irksome. In his side-ward he could inject some flexibility into it without inconveniencing either staff or fellow
patients. (When he was transferred to the main ward, he
continued the pattern as much as he could; for example, he
could read late by the light of his bed lamp, pulling the
curtains partially round the bed to shade other patients
from the light.) So, if he wished, he could watch a late night
movie on his TV and sleep in the next morning. Margaret
brought him his own supply of breakfast cereals ('hospital
cornflakes are the pits'), and the staff would provide him
with a bowl and some milk when he woke.

Then he washed (he could not bath because of the
Hickman Line) or, if he was too weak, he would be washed
by one of the nurses. Once the bed was made and the room
tidied, he listened to a cassette recording, often of a
sermon by John Stott, Rector Emeritus of All Souls
Langham Place, or to the radio. Friends lent him cassettes,
too – some of them light and entertaining for the days when
he could not concentrate on a sermon. On the good days,
some serious reading followed. In the early weeks in hospital he worked through Colin Morris' *God-in-a-Box*, on
the relationship between TV and religion, and John Stott's
large survey of *Issues facing Christians today*. Much later in

his treatment he read a couple of introductions to economics, in order to plug a gap in his general knowledge.

The middle of the day was taken care of by TV news bulletins and the afternoon by a string of novels – the long chunky stories of Leon Uris and Robert Ludlum, thrillers by Len Deighton, Frederick Forsyth and Anthony Price, and a new discovery made at this time, the courtroom mysteries of Michael Gilbert. Evenings usually brought visitors and a wide selection of TV programmes.

Any diversion was welcome. Down in the narrow street below his room he could watch delivery trucks block the entrance to the casualty department, triggering a cacophony of ambulance sirens and car horns; up in the sky he could sometimes see the unusual sight of an Airship Industries' craft wafting across London's rooftops. For exercise, he paced the room at regular intervals, sometimes dragging with him the stanchion which supported bottles or plastic bags drip-feeding into his Hickman Line. The staff helped. Within the limits of their busy workloads they did what they could to inject some humanity into the treatment. The Senior Registrar, Steve Schey, and the nurses sometimes looked in on him just to talk.

The first period of isolation lasted almost three weeks. His spirits brightened once the effects of the chemotherapy wore off, so that by 28 February he was having a heated discussion with his brother Tony about the issues surrounding the British miners' strike, which had already lasted for some months and showed no signs of being resolved.

The following day brought good news. There was no trace of leukaemia in his blood. The inrush of cancer had turned into an equally rapid retreat; the sudden attack had been quickly repelled. His treatment now consisted of just waiting for his neutrophil count to come up, and of occasional top-ups of blood or platelets (an orange-coloured fluid which is the principal blood clotting agent). One night he had a sixteen-hour transfusion which required a nurse to be with him all the time.

Then he developed another infection, establishing a pattern which was to hinder his recovery for months to come. His patience ran low, he became short-tempered and anxious. If his antibiotics – or even the meal trolly – did not appear on schedule, he seemed to feel deserted.

It was a bad infection with a very high temperature. He developed rigors, uncontrollable shaking so violent that the heavy metal-framed bed trembled and rattled. Despite the high temperature he was cold and shivery; he wrapped himself in more clothes. That made him hot; he shed the clothes, turned on the fan, sucked ice cubes and took soluble Panadol.

And then the fog descended on his mind. A dark, dense fog, impenetrable to reason. He felt bleak, desolate.

It was rather like the experience of pain he had after his spleen had been removed twelve years before: it was all-consuming. He could not comprehend that life had not always been like this; he could not conceive of the possibility that there might be life beyond it. He could not even remember his family.

The fog had blanked out his world. He was lost in a void, and he expected to die. The hours of despair crept by like endless days.

Then something grumbled within him; an echo of his determination to fight the evil of cancer reverberated through the thick mist, like the groaning foghorn of an off-shore light vessel guarding treacherous rocks or shoals. And suddenly the fog thinned for an instant; a beam of light followed the sound and swept across his horizon.

'I thought, "I've heard that the leukaemia is on the retreat; I'll be damned if I'm going to get killed off by an infection!" I got really quite angry. And I remembered that I'd been here before, that there was a connection between the depression and the drugs, and that it would come to an end. In the depths of the depression I really understood that I was in God's hands and that there was light at the end of the tunnel. It was remarkable, because you just don't usually get that insight when you are in the depths.'

It was a freak break in the emotional cloud; almost a revelation, some might say. The fog persisted, but now the void was growing lighter. The familiar shapes of his world became first shadows, then solids once again. The depression had lasted for only twelve hours, but it had seemed like an eternity.

A few days later joy completely replaced the sadness. The barrier was lifted on Friday 15 March; for the first time in a fortnight he could kiss Margaret when she arrived. West Ham drew 2-2 with Manchester United in a game televised live, and a bone marrow test showed that the leukaemia was well in retreat. 'It was a good day!' He could look forward to going home soon. He was beginning to crave for a tasty Chinese meal; hospital food had begun to bore him and he had lost his appetite during the chemotherapy.

There was just one snag. The bone marrow test had revealed that the number of blast cells (white cells which have not yet reached full maturity) was one per cent higher than it should have been. This might have been simply because his body was compensating for the chemotherapy, or it might indicate that leukaemia was still present. David Linch, the Consultant, played safe. He gave leukaemia the benefit of the doubt. The original plan had been to give Tim one major course of chemotherapy, followed by a shorter consolidation course which might not involve isolation. But with the blast cell problem, the doctors opted for a second full course before consolidation.

Tim's reprieve from his prison was to be only a brief parole; he was released for forty-eight hours. It just so happened that a teachers' strike had been called at Margaret's school for the same days. Although she was not a member of the striking union, it meant that she could have the days off to spend with Tim at home.

First stop on the journey to Guildford on Tuesday 19 March was the Happy Eater cafe on the A3 trunk road, for 'a good cup of coffee' – and pancakes with maple syrup. In the evening Tim and Margaret had the long-awaited

Chinese meal, shared with Colin Matthews, head of Scripture Union's Bible Use Department, and his wife Jean, which featured in a video about his suffering. Tim monopolised the conversation, largely as a reaction to the weeks of sedation and isolation.

The next morning they went into town. The weather was cold, and his bald head froze. He bought a woollen bobble hat (in the claret and blue colours of West Ham) to keep it warm. He also bought some books to occupy his mind in the coming weeks. Then it was up to the Downs in the afternoon, for a walk across the windswept chalk hills. He could only walk for twenty minutes, but the freedom of the wide open spaces was as much a tonic as a dose of medicine.

That evening he attended the church midweek meeting. Emmanuel, Stoughton, was running a Lent series on the problem of suffering, planned before Tim had developed leukaemia. To have one of their members seriously ill at the same time concentrated their minds more practically on the subject than might otherwise have been the case.

Tim's illness was shared, as it were, by the whole church membership, almost like a fellowship meal. The unlikely starter was a quiche . . .

Seventeen

Friends indeed

The quiche was on the doorstep when Margaret arrived home late after her first visit to Tim in hospital. In the months to come, it was followed by cakes and ready meals for the freezer, supplied by church members so that she would not have to concern herself with preparing and cooking food every day. There were enough invitations to eat out with friends for every meal, if she had been able to accept them all.

Some of the dozen or so people who formed a rota to chauffeur her to and from London, to reduce the added strain of two hours' driving, also provided picnics for her to eat on the journey. The drivers accepted the inconvenience of hanging around in central London for a couple of hours because they could not see Tim personally when he was in isolation, although on Saturdays there was always the additional attraction of the nearby Oxford Street shopping area. Yet another of those many coincidences, which looked much more like a thoughtful piece of God's planning, was that one church member's family firm had premises just behind the Middlesex Hospital – with a private parking space outside. When Margaret did drive herself in at evenings or weekends, she knew that she would always have somewhere to leave the car if the limited public spaces were full.

Tim and Margaret's house had a modest garden which was her special concern; his fingers were never green enough to do more than mow the lawns. The regular hospital visits left her with few springtime and summer evenings to tend it, a fact which she found distressing. But one mother deposited her child for half an hour's piano lesson and then went straight into the garden to prune the many rose bushes. One Saturday morning Margaret got up late to find a neighbour already tidying up her garden; he had thought she was staying in London. As the vague, polite offers of help came in – 'if there's anything we can do, let us know' – Margaret slowly learned to say, 'Yes please'. One weekend a small working party from the church attacked the garden at her request.

Other practical gestures included shopping, and gifts of flowers for both home and hospital. A neighbour turned on the lights in the house at night so that Margaret would return to a welcoming, friendly sight. Some people took their turn with the daily pyjama washing routine, so that Tim always had clean clothes. Others gave money to help defray the mounting cost of Margaret's travel to London – she saw Tim on all but one of his days in hospital, the one she missed being a farewell party at school when she changed jobs. And, of course, there was always someone to feed and water Rockall and Bailey, the rabbits. On two separate occasions, Margaret's parents stayed in the house, looking after practical matters and fielding some of the phone calls.

Work at school was not easy for her in the circumstances; she had no spare time for lesson preparation or for marking students' exercises. But some of the other teachers came to her rescue. One took over her early morning tutorial group to give Margaret a less rushed start to the day. Another asked if she might 'borrow' Margaret's group and combine it with her own for some experimental work; it gave Margaret free time for marking and preparation. Some even marked examination papers for her.

One evening, early in the illness, she noted in her diary: 'Eight practical demonstrations of love in one day! Thank you, Lord.' In Tim and Margaret's words, they were 'bowled over' by the love which was poured out on them. But the greatest impact was made on them by the fact that church members spontaneously organised a twice-weekly prayer meeting for Tim. Each Wednesday evening and Friday morning people prayed together for his healing. On Good Friday the prayer meeting followed on after the special morning service, and about twenty-five people stayed behind to pray.

There had been no time to organise any special public service for Tim this time around, but the volume of prayer offered on their behalf was no less because of it. Church members said that they had been drawn closer to each other as a result of praying and caring for Tim and Margaret. It was a vivid example of the fact that Christian fellowship is a product of Christian love and service, not an entity which can be created and sustained in isolation from other aspects of church life. It meant much to Tim as well as to Margaret; the worry he felt over how she would cope was lifted from his shoulders when he knew that others were looking after her.

The flood of concern poured out by people in Guildford became a torrent as streams of love joined it from around the country, and even from abroad. Margaret was given the key to a friend's flat in central London, so that if she wanted to stay overnight, rather than go home to Guildford, (as she did on some Fridays and Saturdays) she only had to open the door. Other London friends also offered overnight accommodation.

Tim's hospital room brightened up as the days passed, not because the sun shone in, but because the plain walls were gradually covered by a multitude of greetings cards. Friends' children drew him pictures, and they went up on the walls too. Eventually all four walls of his hermit's cell had something tacked on them. When Margaret got home about 10.00 p.m. each night the phone rang non-stop for an hour or more, with people clamouring for news. It was tiring but she never resented it; it was an added assurance that many people cared and were praying.

They were all small things in themselves – a printed card, personalised with a few scribbled words, a postage stamp, a

brief telephone enquiry – but they made a deep impact.
Hours after Tim had broken the news about leukaemia to
David Winter, the broadcaster told a well-known Church
leader with whom Tim had worked on various projects –
and the busy man immediately put a personal letter in the
post, the first contribution to Tim's overflowing mailbag.

It was almost a repeat performance of a dozen years
earlier, when he perhaps had fewer friends and acquaintances, yet was inundated with an almost embarrassing
number of cards and letters. The sense of *déjà vu* was
completed by the volume of visitors to the hospital. When
he had been treated for Hodgkin's Disease he always had at
least one visitor during the official visiting hours, and sometimes several outside hours as well.

Some of these visitors had come as complete surprises.
One day he woke up to find a policeman standing at the foot
of his bed. The officer had once lived near Tim's boyhood
home at Bedfont, and had been best man at Tony Dean's
wedding. He had called in to renew an old acquaintance, in
the process also blocking the already restricted parking
space in the hospital forecourt with his white police Land-
rover.

Another surprise visitor in 1973 had been Hans van
Seventer, who ran the L'Abri Centre in Holland. Tim had
met him while on one of his early visits to the Netherlands,
but he did not know that Hans was in Britain for the arts
students conference which Tim had been due to address.
After the conference Hans made a detour to visit his new
acquaintance in hospital. By 1985 their relationship had
grown. Tim and Margaret had stayed at the Seventer
home, and when he contracted leukaemia the Seventers
wrote and phoned regularly. Such thoughtfulness was
deeply appreciated.

Also from the Netherlands, and just as meaningful, were
the visits of Graham Birtwistle. He too looked in after the
arts students conference in 1973. Twelve years later he was
in Britain for twenty-four hours to give one of the London
Lectures in Contemporary Christianity, and he made his

way again to the Middlesex Hospital. Tim was in isolation, but special dispensation had been given for Graham to see him. Unfortunately Graham had a cold and so could not enter the room. Instead, the two men held a shouted discussion about the lecture through the glass porthole in the heavy wooden door.

It was not the only occasion on which a visitor could merely wave and shout through the glass. People from far afield came to the hospital when they were passing through the capital just to make fleeting eye contact. Among them were figures from the past who had never completely lost touch with Tim. One was Nick Brotherwood, the former drummer for Screw (the warm-up band before the Rolling Stones' free concert in Hyde Park), down from Nottingham where he was a curate at St Nicholas' Church.

Being confronted by someone who is seriously ill is not, of course, an easy experience to cope with. Not everyone in Tim's circle of contacts was sure how to react. When a work colleague stands up in the office to make a public announcement that he has leukaemia, or when the fact is stated without prior warning during the intercessions in a Sunday morning church service, what do you do, what can you say?

Some of the Elm House staff and some of the Emmanuel congregation slipped quietly away, unable to say anything to him personally, unable even to look him in the face, to offer him a token gesture of support. They were aware, perhaps, of the futility of polite words; conscious, perhaps, of their own mortality and their inability to come to terms with it; embarrassed, even, by such a devastatingly frank and intimate revelation. Later on, even simple questions such as 'How are you?' were sometimes asked through third parties rather than directly to Tim. Faced with the unknown or the unexpected we hold the source of our confusion at arm's length; but what shall we do when it strikes our arm?

Aware of the confusion and uncertainty which can afflict friends and relatives of patients, Tim did what he could

during both illnesses to put them at ease. He often took the
initiative about the progress of the illness and its treatment,
occasionally boring his listeners with unnecessary detail,
but the therapeutic benefit which it gave him also removed
any reticence the visitors might have felt about broaching
the subject.

His own openness made him more acutely aware of the
extent to which the difficulties and pressures which people
face are hushed up even within the Church. For example,
couples can be experiencing strain in their marriage but no
one knows until it is too late. A simple (and anonymous)
prayer request may be all that is required to open up the
discussions and stimulate the practical concern; 'hushing
up is unhealthy'.

After his leukaemia treatment, Tim went with Margaret
to a church, preached, and then had a 'no questions barred'
come-back session afterwards. People seemed almost desperate to talk openly about the practical details of coping
with suffering of all kinds. And to those who are apologetic
about 'making a fuss' about their own problems, Tim says,
'Any pain is important even if it seems "nothing like you've
got". It is important to the person who suffers it.'

When a person is in hospital, the world outside continues
as if he or she were irrevelant to it. So the patient's state of
health should not be the only topic of conversation at the
bedside. For Tim, it was important that his visitors told him
what they had been doing during the day, or shared their
concerns and opinions about current issues – just as they
would if they had met for a sandwich lunch on a park bench.
'It's possible to so classify the person as a patient that they
become dismembered.'

Of course, there are times when the patient is too ill or
too tired to talk, and that was a frequent state of affairs for
Tim, especially during the chemotherapy for leukaemia.
Silence can create awkwardness; people fidget, become
embarrassed, think of trivial things to say, or make excuses
to slip away early. Sometimes, however, the patient just
needs the physical presence of another person. Margaret

often took her knitting and simply sat with Tim. At times, 'I wouldn't have been bothered if someone had got a book out and begun reading.' Steve Nickless, one of the four outsiders allowed in during the isolation, visited Tim most evenings around 6.00 p.m. When Tim was feeling low, they just sat and watched the TV news together; when he was totally flattened by the treatment, they just sat.

It was a measure of the strength of Job's three friends that when they first visited the man who had lost everything, 'they sat on the ground with him for seven days and seven nights. No one said a word to him, because they saw how great his suffering was,' (Job 2:13). It was their weakness that they then began prattling about a theology of suffering which they did not understand, offering slick spiritual prescriptions for a profoundly complex problem to a person who was in no fit state to apply his mind to abstruse philosophy.

Tim had, and has, only one message for the people who wished to preach glib sermons about how to be healed, or who come to the bedside with a burning desire to 'minister' to the patient, but are who are not also willing to empathise with him: 'Please stay clear of the bed.' Ministry, to be meaningful, must grow out of deep mutual trust and personal involvement.

There is another sort of visitor who also needs to avoid the sick person: the one who is so burdened by their own problems that they are unable to contain them. During his Hodgkin's treatment one woman used her captive audience as an almost daily sounding board for her complaints. Drained of his emotional and physical strength, Tim eventually phoned a mutual friend and asked him to exert some restraint on the frequency and length of her visits.

Otherwise, the sheer presence of people was encouraging and stimulating during both illnesses. One delightful experience came when a man Tim had never met before began to visit him, often content to wave through the door when the barrier was down. He had heard about Tim in a prayer meeting with Roger Simpson, Tim's 'chaplain'. He worked nearby, and just came along to say 'Hello'. 'You should never underestimate the value of making hospital visits. They were incredibly important to me, just seeing people.'

Looking back years later on the Hodgkin's period, with its spontaneous birthday party, the cards and the many visitors, Tim still felt indebted. 'I had so much love poured out on me that it was almost more than I could endure. I got really choked thinking that people cared so much.'

It was the kind of experience which makes a man feel as tall as the Eiffel Tower, yet as small as a fly on the wall. It makes him conscious that he is Man, and convinced that he is mortal. Although such a thing can never be quantified, it must have had an important bearing on his eventual recovery. 'Pleasant words are a honeycomb, sweet to the soul and healing to the bones' (Prov. 16:24).

It also gave a whole new dimension to the description of the Church as 'the body of Christ'. According to the New Testament, it means being 'devoted to one another in brotherly love . . . Share with God's people who are in need . . . Rejoice with those who rejoice; mourn with those who mourn.' It is an egalitarian, not a hierarchical, group, so 'that there may be no division in the body, but that its parts should have equal concern for each other. If one part suffers, every part suffers with it; if one part is honoured, every part rejoices with it' (Rom. 12:10, 13, 15; 1 Cor. 12: 25, 26).

While on the receiving end of such care, Tim realised that 'one of the most important gifts God has given to the world is the caring Church, who say to humanity, "We as the body of Christ are the representatives of God's acts in history." We have to demonstrate that our acts are the acts of God. What I experienced in hospital is in turn now an indictment of me and my ministry (or lack of it) to others.'

An equally loving response from people when he had leukaemia prompted him to make some searching comments about those who are not so fortunate. He and Margaret were:

. . . surrounded by strong caring groups: our Christian families; neighbours; a lively thoughtful and prayerful Church giving us practical support; a workplace where colleagues prayed, worked to keep the magazine going, and provided my full salary throughout; and lastly a wide network of friends, acquaintances and other Churches that showed their love in words and deeds. All gifts of God indeed. All contributing to our well-being and the alleviation of unnecessary worries and concerns.

In looking for support in every group that surrounds me, I could ask for no more . . . for some, though, the situation is quite different. What of the person who contracts cancer when the picture looks quite different: no family, or a hostile home. Unhelpful neighbours. No caring community such as a Church (or else a Church that is dead). Maybe they are unemployed, or in a job where sick pay is inadequate and financial worries won't go away. What if relatives can't cope? What if friends and relatives are few – and the victim is in hospital miles from home (as I was) where access is difficult and limited? This may be at the other extreme, yet all those dimensions are experienced by some. It is, to me, no wonder that Jesus cites caring for the sick as a sign of righteousness.'[1]

So it was, as part of the two-way fellowship of Christians, that on Wednesday 20 March 1985, during his forty-eight hour break between courses of chemotherapy, Tim went to Emmanuel, Stoughton, for the mid-week meeting. He sat at the back; he was not allowed to mix closely with people because of the risk of infection. After the first hymn he walked forward to the lectern.

He thanked the people for their prayer and practical concern, and told them how the treatment was progressing. He added that he was praying for them, too, that they would be united and that the love of Christ would be seen among them. And then he went straight home. The sight of his bald head and smooth chin, and his obvious willingness to open up the subject and build bridges of his own to people, moved and challenged many who were present.

It was the first of two occasions when he was to address the whole Church about his condition. The second occasion was to come three months later. His message then was to have a very different complexion. With the passage of time, his condition moved into almost virgin medical territory.

And the treatment became harder to cope with.

Eighteen

Reaction – and refreshment

The second course of chemotherapy began the day Tim returned to hospital, Thursday 21 March. He reported to the ward in the afternoon, and negotiated to have the drugs late in the evening. That gave him a little more time out, an opportunity to have one last meal with friends before he sank into the narcotic delirium which he was not looking forward to at all.

It came quickly, accompanied by a savage infection. On Sunday his temperature had shot to the upper safety limits and the ice cubes and fan were brought into action. He was very sick and could only take his pills if they were ground up in milk. Tony Dean was not so fit, either; he hobbled in with a walking stick to see his brother, having hurt his back.

By Tuesday his temperature was down and his mind was more alert. He finished Leon Uris' *The Haj*, read a chapter of Stott's *Issues*, and listened to a tape. But he was still very doped and his words and movements were desperately slow.

And on Wednesday he developed a form of Parkinson's Disease. His body shook constantly, not with the violence of the rigors he had when running a fever, but with the weakness of a frail old person. Dr Jelliffe came to see him, and thought it might be the result of tension. Tim thought differently, and so did Marilyn Marks. She was a hospital sister, not in uniform, who worked as an oncology (cancer) counsellor. She suggested that it was a side-effect of the anti-sickness drugs, and she was proved right. Tim was taken off them.

He was given other drugs to combat the Parkinson's Disease. They reacted with something else and brought him out in a total body rash. Now he itched all over, and was not allowed to scratch. For Tim, the equivalent of the pottery fragment with which the biblical Job scraped his sores was calamine lotion. The temptation to scratch was not his only problem; the drugs had also given him blurred and double vision.

The worst reactions were over by the time the barrier came down on Friday night, 29 March, and he was in isolation again. On Sunday evening a nurse brought him the chemotherapy and he refused to take it. Like a castaway on a desert island notching up the passing days on a palm tree, he had counted the doses. He knew that he had finished the course and insisted that the nurse go and check. She found the ambiguous note left by the doctors. It said 'last chemo 31 March' but did not add 'morning only' as it should have done. Tim was right.

Now it was a matter of waiting for the neutrophil count to come up sufficiently to allow him to take his place in the wide world again. At least, it should have been. On Tuesday 2 April a viral infection inflamed his throat and ulcerated his mouth. He could not swallow anything. He tried sucking ice cubes, which helped once the burning sensation they initially produced on his tongue had died away. Like a desert traveller imagining oases, he began to fantasise about drinks. Images of 'great drinks I have known' flashed across his mind, starting with an out-of-this-world *cappucino* he had enjoyed in Koblenz the previous year.

Then came one of those days all married couples experience, when one is floating high and the other is sinking low. Thursday 4 April – Maundy Thursday – was Margaret's last day of teaching at her school. She had been appointed Diocesan Children's Education Officer for five to twelve year olds in Sunday schools and church day schools for the Church of England's Guildford Diocese. It was to make her summer term – usually the busiest for a teacher – much easier: another providential piece of help which had been decided before Tim fell ill.

She went home that afternoon, laden with farewell gifts from children and staff alike: a miniature rose, daffodils, a bouquet, pot plants, boxes of chocolates, a shell vase, a pair of secateurs, a flower book, a picture, three records and a cake. That evening she drove to the hospital to find that her husband had been in tears for most of the day.

His throat and mouth were still sore; he could sip only weak blackcurrant juice. He was very tired. And when he had been given drugs that morning to tackle the virus, he vomited them out. Instantly he went back in time to the days of his aversion to CCNU. The old worries tore into his mind like stampeding steers. He needed the drugs in order to live, yet he could not bear to take them. He cried on the ward sister's shoulder.

The strain of not being able to touch Margaret became unbearable. He pleaded for some way in which he could hold and hug her. To be close to the woman he loved, yet forbidden even a brief embrace, was something akin to Chinese water torture.

The ward sister, Beverley Cornish, had a bright idea. The wonder was that someone had not thought of it before. They gave Margaret an operating theatre gown, which completely covered her clothes, as well as the usual mask and gloves. Physical contact was restored; Tim's spirits brightened slowly. The staff also discovered that the drugs were available in a liquid suspension, so the episode was not repeated.

On Easter Sunday he was feeling better. In the morning he listened to the whole of Handel's *Messiah* on tape, an uplifting experience lasting two and a half hours. He always tried to keep Sunday as different as he could. Sometimes the Salvation Army band passed by the hospital, their live music creating a bridge between him and the outside world and filling the air with notes of assurance; he was not alone but was still in the hands of his caring heavenly Father. Roger Simpson usually came in and they had holy communion together.

He tuned into broadcast services, too. One Sunday he saw James Jones, with whom he had shared media studies lectures at Trinity College, preaching at a service from Bristol on BBC 1. On ITV, Myra Blyth (a contributor to *Third Way*) and hospital free church chaplain John Newton were leading worship. And in the evening, Sally Magnusson, Norman Stone's wife, presented *Songs of Praise* on BBC 1. The TV had brought his friends to his room, and they shared in worship together.

After Easter, Tim was desperately keen to get home. As each day passed, he felt brighter and fitter. His desire for freedom was not simply because he was fed up with isolation. It was also because he had worked, prayed, planned and in a sense lived for some important meetings which were about to take place.

The 1984 London Lectures in Contemporary Christianity (dated 1984 but not given until 1985 to accommodate the diary of one of the speakers) were due to begin on 11 April. The theme was 'Art in question', and the first lecturer was Graham Birtwistle, who shouted the substance of his talk through the hospital door. The doctors had told Tim that he might be out in time for the next one (15 April), but his neutrophil count refused to rise to the required level. It was frustrating in the extreme; having been one of the organisers, he wanted to be in on the event itself.

What hurt even more was that he had to miss a private consultation at the House of Commons on 16 April. Organised by Tim, David Winter of the BBC and John Stott, and hosted by them and Welsh Labour MP Donald Anderson, it brought together church leaders, theologians, media people and MPs from all parties, for a frank off-the-record discussion about the responsibilities of the media. It was a strategic event.

For two hours Tim paced his room waiting to hear if the blood count was sufficiently high to allow him out for the day. By a rare oversight the result of the test, which had been taken early with this possibility in view, was not communicated to him for some while after it was known, which added to the tension. The count was too low, however, for him to leave isolation and the meeting went ahead without him. His disappointment was intense, spilling over into anger. The coincidence did not happen when he most wanted it to; God had not removed all mystery and difficulty from his purpose for Tim, even if he had often smoothed the way in the past.

At last the magic day came. His neutrophil count leapt overnight to a point well in excess of the safety margin. Sunday 21 April: free at last! Since 18 February he had spent sixty days in hospital, forty of them in isolation. Margaret lunched with John Salter, vicar of Emmanuel, and his wife Bridget, and all three went to collect Tim in the afternoon. They made the standard stop on the journey back: the Happy Eater on the A3, where at 3.30 p.m. Tim, his palate drooling for different food, tucked into an all-day breakfast of sausage, egg, baked beans and fried bread. When he went to the evening service, and John Salter announced his presence, the church erupted with applause.

There can be few instances in a person's life which can compare to the *joie de vivre*, the exultant gladness, which surges through someone who is released from captivity. The little things of life, perhaps regarded once as chores, become positive delights. The world looks young and fresh again; there is so much to do, so many people to see. Tim could look forward to a week at home before he went back for the consolidation course, which was likely to be more of a minor irritation than a major exercise. Rejoicing in his freedom, he launched into life again.

Food, which had occupied his thoughts in hospital, now occupied his time at home, and he cooked many of the meals that week. One day, he just fancied making bread, so he did. And he and Margaret took two Guildford couples out to an Indian restaurant as a 'thank you' for their special help.

There were other, older friends to see. They drove to Hampshire to see David and Tricia Porter; David had just given one of the London Lectures. They held a dinner party for Tony and Diana Hudson, and Tony and Sue Wales, together with Paul Clowney, who had been Tim's successor at UCCF, and his wife Tessa. To say nothing of attending a nephew's birthday party, paying a visit to the office, and making a trip to the cinema to see *A Passage To India* – preceded by a hamburger in a Wimpy Bar. At one point in the week Margaret began to think that Tim's energy exceeded hers. And once again, the timing had been just right for her; she was not due to begin her new job until May, and so could spend the week with him.

But on 30 April it was back to the Middlesex, this time with a huge jar of sweets for the nurses, another 'thank you' gesture. The sweets went down well, literally; one nurse tipped them all on the floor as she groped for an elusive sugared almond.

Tony and Verity also visited the hospital the same day for tests, to see if their bone marrow was compatible with Tim's. If it was, and if after the consolidation course there was no further sign of leukaemia, he might be given a bone marrow transplant, using either his sister or brother as a donor, to provide a 'gilt edged' insurance against developing the cancer again.

There were no problems associated with the consolidation course. The only hitch was that he did not arrive home after being discharged a week later until 11.30 p.m. The platelets he required were given to someone else in an emergency, and he had to wait some hours for a new supply and a doctor to administer them via the Hickman Line.

The next couple of weeks were occupied by a series of visits to the Middlesex for blood tests and one overnight stay for a transfusion. But now the finishing straight looked close at hand. The time had come for recuperating, and for picking up the threads of normal life which had been laid aside so hastily three months before. The bone marrow transplant, which was not without its risks, would be the final hurdle to clear.

Realising that it was impossible to respond personally to all the messages of love, encouragement and support which they had received, Tim and Margaret mailed out a circular letter to 300 people at the end of May, thanking them for their support and updating them on progress. Typically, it was not without humour, and of a kind which, to those who did not know the couple, might have seemed warped or even insensitive. Norman Stone provided a cartoon of Tim wired up to a large 'automatic blood tester and sampler'. The doctor who was standing by held a small test tube, and pointing to it said: 'First the good news . . . this is the blood you can keep!'

Humour of that kind can add depth of field to the human vision, which has so focussed on the close-up detail that the background context has become blurred. There can be genuine laughter in the midst of pain, helping the sufferer to stand outside himself for a moment. And it proves that the old proverb is not without its truth: laughter is a good, if not the best, medicine.

Then Tim and Margaret packed their bags and went off for a holiday at the end of May; no one could deny that they deserved it. But even that was not simply an ice cream interval during a scene change in their drama; it was thickly woven into the plot.

It happened because Tim had made a new friend in Bill Edgar, one of the London Lecturers, as they prepared for the series. Bill, an American, lived with his wife Barbara in the South of France, and taught apologetics at a Reformed theological seminary in Aix-en-Provence. When he heard that Tim had leukaemia, he phoned from France and said, 'I know it sounds stupid, but if there's anything we can do, let us know.'

There was, of course. The treatment had been a strain for both Tim and Margaret, and Tim, although feeling well, was still tired and he had lost twenty-eight pounds in weight. They needed a holiday, a complete break away from it all, and they phoned the Edgars to see if they could stay with them. It was no sooner said than arranged. British friends paid for their flight to Marseilles, and others anonymously sent the Edgars money so that they could introduce the couple to the local French cuisine, as an aid to the physical and emotional recovery process.

So Tim and Margaret were treated to a total change of culture. They explored the city's small squares lined with plane trees, watched the many dancing fountains, and saw where the painter Cezanne had lived, worked and died. They borrowed Bill's car and discovered why the area has the second worse accident rate in the whole of France; street signs seemed to have been erected more for decoration than obedience. They motored to the St Victoire mountains, where Gauguin had painted, and down to the fjord-like coastline. And one night Bill took them to a jazz club where he, the American Presbyterian clergyman, missionary and lecturer, played once a month in his own band, Le Swing Jazz Group, with three Frenchmen who were not Christians.

There was one dark spot in the otherwise bright week. It appeared on their first full day in Aix. They drove with Bill and Barbara Edgar to Avignon, where according to the song all the world is supposed to have danced *sur le pont*. On the drive home both Tim, sitting in the front, and Margaret, in the back, were subdued. As they talked together that night, they discovered that each had been filled with foreboding at about the same time: this could be their last holiday together.

They banished the thought. Should Tim be given a short life sentence if leukaemia returned, they would go on another holiday first, probably to the Netherlands which Margaret had come to love as much as Tim. They would not live always in such fear; they determined to enjoy the life God gave them first, and cross that *pont* when they got to it.

The incident illustrated the rather obvious fact that while Tim had suffered, so too had Margaret. In certain respects she had the harder task; she could only sit and watch, helplessly.

Her natural patience and equable temperament had taken a hammering. Her deep affection for her husband had only served to increase her pain.

Nineteen

One flesh, one spirit

Tim and Margaret could not have been more different in character. While he was listening to the Rolling Stones in Hyde Park, London, in the 1960s, she was playing Beethoven sonatas down on the south coast of England. He was unorthodox in dress and lifestyle, she fitted happily into the orthodox stereotype of a vicar's daughter. He was strong-willed and determined, expounding his definite views and attacking contrary opinions vigorously; she, although not one to suffer fools gladly, had a woman's sensitivity to human weakness which modifies public confrontation. He was talkative, she was quieter; he was given to peaks of enthusiasm and troughs of depression; she was more even keeled and rarely experienced the extremes of emotion.

But like gear wheels forged for each other, they meshed rather than clashed; like a picture sliced in half, the two sides matched when brought together. If he ever had been a real life incarnation of Goscinny's Timandahalf in the Asterix story, with Margaret at his side he immediately shrank to normal dimensions and grew to greater wholeness.

Curious, at first, about the man she often heard people speak of in the UCCF environment, she discovered that beneath the skin of the fluent speaker, the efficient organiser and the broad thinker, lay a fun-loving and sensitive person who could be cut to the raw by the criticism he sometimes invited. His personal warmth and honesty, combined with his habit of total commitment to people and causes, testified to an integrity she could respect and trust.

Far from finding their interests at variance, they taught each other new things and found the experience satisfying. They became very good friends, and fell in love.

Although upset by the initial realisation that he would drag Margaret through the hellish corridors of chemotherapy for his leukaemia, her steady presence during the often dark days provided Tim with a resource he had not had in the treatment for Hodgkin's Disease, and which he found in the event to be indispensable: 'the daily continual presence of the person you love by your side is indescribably important.'

That person, too, fought her own unique battles in such a situation. The practical help she received made life considerably easier for her, but that could never directly relieve the anxiety and at times bewilderment which struck her. She found that it was important to have people to whom she could unburden herself, but they had to be people of her own choosing. A few, it seemed, almost wanted (perhaps, in a sense, because of their own problems, they almost needed) her to cry on their shoulders. They prefaced their hints with statements such as, 'You're wonderful! I don't know how you cope!' To which, on some occasions, she made her point in jest by replying, 'Yes, I know I am and I don't know how I cope either!'

In fact, she did cope because, like Tim, she had a deep assurance that they were both firmly in God's loving hands. An unsought-for sense of the presence of God remained with her throughout his illness. At times God's support was so real to her that she almost felt she could touch him. 'It reduced me to a quivering heap that he should be so caring to an insignificant creature like me, who happens to have a husband who is ill.' Church services were sometimes emotional experiences, not usually because she was upset about Tim but because the reminders of God's reality made the gratitude to him just well up inside her.

Alongside the awareness of God she also experienced an unusual assurance. The twenty-third Psalm became especially meaningful to her.

> Even though I walk
>   through the valley of the shadow of death,
> I will fear no evil,
>   for you are with me;
> your rod and your staff
>   they comfort me (Ps. 23:4).

The emphasis was on the word *through*. The verse was a powerful picture of a stage in a journey, not its terminus. With that proper level of agnosticism which prevents true faith from becoming brash, yet which never slides into doubt, she believed that Tim would be pulled through the crisis.

She was not alone in that intuitive conviction; others shared it too. David Porter, who does not come from the Christian tradition which readily plucks promises from scripture by prophetic discernment, none the less felt constrained to remind Tim of one: 'For I know the plans I have for you, says the Lord, plans for welfare and not for evil, to give you a future and a hope' (Jer. 9:11, RSV). And Tim's brother Tony, who reckoned that Tim had survived Hodgkin's Disease only through prayer, also had a strong feeling that he would not succumb to the second cancer on which he had declared war.

Such feelings can of course be wishful thinking superimposed over the true picture of God's purposes; they can perhaps also be a God-given source of strength for the battle rather than a definitive statement about the future.

But Margaret had also experienced an odd sensation when Tim came home early that night to break the news about leukaemia. Deep inside her some flame of recognition flickered. 'It was almost,' she reflected later, 'as if a hidden hunch had been revealed. I realised, "Here we are; this is what I thought might happen." It was a strange sensation.' Especially when it is remembered that she had not been plagued by fear of a return of Hodgkin's Disease.

Whence came that whisper of knowingness none can tell. The cynic cites repressed fear; the sceptic suggests woman's intuition; and the believer sees the caring hand of God reaching through the chaos to cushion the blow. But whatever the source, it cushioned the blow only lightly.

What did help her come to terms with the facts quickly was Tim's openness, and especially the telephone marathon before he went into hospital. She expected at first that the constant repetition of the story (the telephone is in the hallway, and it would have been impossible for her to have gone totally out of earshot without also leaving the house) would really upset her. In fact, it familiarised her with reality; the story became commonplace.

She did not then sail through the stormy months of watching and waiting with all the grace and ease of a tall ship racing with the wind. The emotional strain and physical tiredness of a daily journey after work took its toll. She walked away from one teacher who had rather thoughtlessly told her she had 150 reports to write, and promptly burst into tears in front of another. When one class was being particularly difficult, she could take no more and walked out on them, too; they were so shocked that when she came back five minutes later they were on their best behaviour.

She also found that she was affected by Tim's moods and often reflected them. Rather than being able to cheer him up when he felt down, she became subdued as well. But while that distressed her, the empathy which resulted from it was probably more valuable to Tim than any artificial humour or lightness. His physical and mental deterioration hurt her deeply, and she was profoundly thankful that she had been warned in advance that the drugs would have such an effect – and that the effect would wear off in time. The anxiety and frustration felt by a loving spouse in such circumstances was neatly illustrated by one entry in her diary: 'I long to know what you're thinking – but I know you don't feel up to talking.'

Isolation was no more easy for her than it was for him.

The plastic mask, apron and gloves made her very hot and uncomfortable in the warm hospital. When she was given the operating theatre gown so she could hug Tim, the delight was dampened a little by the increased discomfort. One Saturday she just had to break her visit in half and go out for a walk and some fresh air. But never once did she leave the hospital with anything but a feeling of reluctance and sadness. However uncomfortable, it was the only place she really wanted to be; at least she could be thankful that they were not separated by a sheet of glass.

At times, though, it seemed as though they were; she felt like an observer, looking on from a distance. It protected her from despair, but she felt it was a peculiar emotion to have towards the person she loved. The distance was increased by her physical helplessness. There was little she could do in practical terms for him. His care was in the hands of an efficient and skilled team of doctors and nurses, and she was reduced to the status of a spectator who could occasionally go on small errands for the performer. She did not resent their work – they did everything they could to ensure that she was welcomed and kept fully informed – but true love can never be content to sit idly by when the beloved is suffering or in need.

Occasionally doubt – or at least uncertainty – threatened her assurance that Tim would pull through. The thought that she might have to live alone was devastating when it broke through her defences. Quite what God was doing in the twists and turns of the tortuous path to healing was a total mystery. And on their wedding anniversary she could not help but pray that there might be another to celebrate.

But that was in July, six weeks after their holiday in France. It had been a good holiday; Tim put on fourteen pounds in weight and regained his zest for work on *Third Way*. After the break, although not officially back at work, he went into the office several times.

Then on Thursday June 20 he went with Margaret to see David Linch, the Consultant, about the final stages of treatment. And they received a message far different from the one they had expected.

Twenty

The writing on the wall

Tim and Margaret sat in David Linch's office at the Middlesex Hospital. They expected to be told that Tim would have a bone marrow transplant. The leukaemia was in complete remission, but like a bad penny could possibly turn up again without warning. A transplant was as close to a guarantee as possible at the time that the disease would not recur.

The bone marrow would be taken either from Tim's brother Tony or sister Verity. Only siblings are likely to have the exact tissue match. To find a donor outside the family with an exact match in all details would be a task equivalent to that of looking for a needle in a haystack. Even if the major factors corresponded, differences in minor detail could reduce the effectiveness of the operation. If neither Tony nor Verity could supply suitable bone marrow, then the doctors could do a 'clean up' operation on Tim's own, by removing it, treating it and then replacing it in an 'autologous transplant'.

David Linch faced them across the desk. Tim's brother and sister, he said, did not have the correct tissue match.

And Tim did have a monocytic condition. The level of his monocyte white cells was still higher than normal. It was not leukaemia, but a pre-leukaemia condition. Even if the doctors did an autologous transplant, the condition would probably remain.

He used very strong terms: 'The future is very bleak for you.' He explained that there had only been one other case in Britain of someone who had suffered acute myeloid leukaemia secondary to Hodgkin's Disease, who had then developed a monocytic condition after the remission of the leukaemia.

'We are working entirely in the dark,' the Consultant said. 'I can't guarantee that what we propose to do will work.' If it did not, then the decisions would be in Tim's hands. If leukaemia recurred, he would have to choose between further chemotherapy which might – or might not – lengthen his life for a while, with all the attendant hassles of isolation, or a truncated but less traumatic life.

Tim and Margaret called it the writing on the wall speech. The leering jaws of death had only slunk back into the undergrowth, it seemed, crouching, waiting for another chance to snap at their intended victim.

The following Sunday Margaret was away at another church in connection with her Diocesan job. At Emmanuel, Stoughton, Tim went to the front during the notices and for the second time in a matter of months addressed the congregation about his health. He told them what David Linch had said, and asked them to pray for himself and Margaret. He faltered momentarily as the tears came to his eyes. Then he added: 'Don't worry. I'm due to preach in that pulpit on the first of September on the raising of Lazarus – and I will!' The congregation laughed, although the humour in his voice had not been pre-meditated. He asked for an extra hymn to be sung, to lift people's minds at once from the temporal uncertainties to eternal absolutes: *Jesus is Lord! Creation's voice proclaims it* . . .

Jesus is Lord! Jesus is Lord!
Praise him with 'Hallelujahs' for Jesus is Lord!

The proposed treatment consisted of two further courses of chemotherapy, shorter than the main anti-leukaemia courses and probably not involving isolation. David Linch had recommended that the first one begin as soon as possible, so Tim was back on the main Greenhow Ward on

Tuesday 25 June. It lasted for a week, but it meant that he had to miss yet another meeting he had worked on – a media weekend conference organised by the London Institute for Contemporary Christianity – and the wedding in Guildford the same weekend of the church member whose family firm had provided the parking space behind the hospital.

The treatment was civilised and the side-effects nil. Tim was able to read, and even work. Although Veronica Zundel had taken over the day to day running of *Third Way* in his extended absence, he had held on to two projects associated with the magazine and which, like the London Lectures and the House of Commons consultation, he wanted to live to see through.

One was a series of books published by SPCK in association with *Third Way*. 'Third Way Books' provided an opportunity to examine in some depth issues which a magazine could broach only broadly. Tim had acted as series editor, dealing with authors and their manuscripts. The first three titles were due to be published in the autumn.[1] So while Tim was on the first of the new courses of treatment, designer Philip Miles (who had been one of the speakers at the arts conference in 1973 which Tim had missed . . .) and SPCK editor Judith Longman visited the hospital to discuss with him the rough cover designs which they spread over his bed. The other project was the first *Third Way* lecture, due to be given in September, to extend the ministry of the magazine beyond the printed page, and to provide the rare opportunity within the media for producers and readers to get together.

It was Margaret's birthday just before the second course of treatment began (there was a week's break between the two courses), and their wedding anniversary would fall while Tim was in hospital. They combined the celebrations while he was still at large. They saw *The Witness*, at a cinema in the nearby town of Farnham, and Tom Stoppard's comedy *Jumpers* at a theatre in London. Strolling through Covent Garden on their way to *Jumpers* they paused to enjoy a special display of foolery by many clowns; afterwards they enlarged their knowledge of international menus by dining in an American restaurant.

A few days later the gaiety of the weekend had faded and the world looked grey again. Tim had not been looking forward to going into hospital, and on this occasion Greenhow Ward was almost like a morgue. Hardly any of the patients were mobile. One man's throat had been removed and, not surprisingly, he was feeling depressed. In the middle of the night another patient, two beds away from Tim, began screaming, 'I want to die! I want to die!' He did die, the next morning, and far from peacefully.

And Tim had rejected his drugs again – twice. He had been feeling unwell, and the effort of swallowing pills proved too much for him. The second time he was sick, however, they had been crushed in milk, which made the reaction all the more worrying for him. But he completed the treatment, and the signs that it was achieving its intended purpose were good.

Tim, however, had not seen the last of the hospital. He made a routine visit at the beginning of August, but as he had developed an ulcerated tongue and a throat infection he was kept in for treatment for a week. This time he had a normal temperature and was able to go out of hospital from time to time. A friend from Cyprus came to see him, and they went out for lunch together. One evening he walked round St James's Park with friends; they sat watching the ducks in the darkness and listening to the wartime sounds from a *son et lumière* performance in nearby Horseguard's Parade.

At the end of August he had another infection, accompanied by an almost bizarre train of events. He had returned to work officially on 19 August, and after three days was already feeling unwell. He went to the hospital for a check up but they saw no reason to keep him in. They reckoned he had had a mild dose of flu. He was glad; he wanted to be at the Greenbelt Festival the following weekend. Tim was due to take part in a dialogue with Graham

Cray, David Watson's successor as Rector of St Michael le Belfrey church in York. Their subject was the Christian attitude to war. Tim supported the 'just war' theory and Graham Cray took the non-violent resistance approach.

The hospital allowed him to go away that weekend after reporting to them on Friday morning. A few hours after he had left, the doctors found that they had grown a virulent bug in the blood culture they had taken from him. They wanted him back fast but could not remember where he was going. They telephoned his home, but there was no answer. They telephoned Margaret's office, and the secretary said that they had already left. She did not say, nor was she asked, where they had gone. Then a Christian doctor who was one of the team treating him remembered that he was at Greenbelt. She sent a message via Malcolm and Meryl Doney, who had not yet left London, that Tim was to go back to the hospital. But their car broke down, and they reached Greenbelt too late to tell Tim, who had by then already gone home.

Tim felt quite well to begin with, and was unaware of any need to return. The dialogue was a success. It illustrated how two Christians could disagree on an important question without resorting to verbal violence, and could retain their love and respect for one another.

After it, he began to feel unwell and so he went home. By Monday he was feeling rough. He phoned the hospital to tell them he was coming in, and was driven to London by a friend. The doctors knew he would turn up some time: he had septicaemia (blood poisoning).

He became very ill. The fever grew worse and he developed rigors. He was given the antibiotics he usually took. He prayed they would work. Sunday 1 September was only days away. That was his date to preach from the Emmanuel pulpit. He had promised he would be there.

And the gospel story of the raising of Lazarus had made a big impact on him during his treatment for leukaemia. He wanted to share his insights with the congregation which had supported him and Margaret so helpfully.

Twenty-One

Jesus wept

Death is not a pleasant subject; to observers it frequently appears not to be a pleasant experience. It is usually and quite literally the last thing we talk about. We whisk it away rapidly in quiet limousines and swiftly and silently consign it to the unseen furnace beyond the crematorium's velvet curtains. Relatives at a funeral are expected to be 'brave', which means behaving much as if they were at one of those dutiful family reunions where everyone is painfully polite and falsely jovial. Tears are regarded as a temporary lapse of self-control, to be quickly dried because 'life must go on'.

Which makes Jesus's behaviour at the tomb of his friend Lazarus refreshing and, for mourners, comforting: 'Jesus wept' (John 11: 1–44). Yet it was a strange incident riddled with questions. Why did he take so long before going to the scene? And once there, already knowing that he would bring Lazarus back to life again, why did he shed tears?

One night, as Tim lay awake in his hospital room during the chemotherapy for leukaemia, he wrestled with those questions during an hours-long cocktail of prayer, thought and Bible study. Two things struck him with renewed power and insight, which helped him to understand – and bear – his predicament further. They also gave him the raw material for his promised sermon at Emmanuel.

The first was that Jesus no doubt did share the grief of the mourners, identified with their pain and so wept with those who weep. But the root cause of his tears was something else – something which Bible translators have never found easy to express in English. Most versions have something like 'he was deeply moved in spirit and troubled'; in other words, he was upset that his friend was dead.

But the words mean more than that. 'He was moved with indignation' (Living Bible); 'he chafed in spirit' (Moffat). 'To chafe' is to become angry. Jesus was not just mournful, he was angry.

And so was Tim. 'One thing kept me smiling as I fought leukaemia, and that was knowing that Jesus was angry. I was angry, especially when infection hit me after the leukaemia was in retreat. I was angry, and so was Jesus, against the sickness.' The cancer was not simply an accident, but was a manifestation of the evil which corrupts the world. Anger against such an evil – not against God – was, Tim realised, a perfectly proper emotion to feel.

Jesus's anger was that of a righteous God who sees the vandalism which has turned the garden of Eden into an overgrown cemetery; he recognises death for what it is: the ultimate obscenity. 'Jesus sees the profanity and blasphemy of death and its root cause in sin, because it has the audacity to strike down Lazarus who is made in the image of God. Death is not like chopping down trees; there's something precious in everyone. And Jesus sees through to its cause – the sin that plagues all of us.'

God never desired that human dust should return to the dust from which it was taken; he had a far nobler purpose than that for the human race whom he appointed co-rulers of the good earth he had made. Human sin put paid to that, and the 'fall' brought death as well as disease and disintegration. That was a situation which God could not allow to continue for ever. He had to do something about it, and he did it through Christ, first at the tomb of Lazarus, and then on his own cross.

It is death that is the object of his wrath, and behind death him who has the power of death, and whom he has come into the world to destroy. Tears of sympathy may fill his eyes, but this is incidental. His soul is held by rage:

and he advances to the tomb, in Calvin's words, 'as a champion who prepares for conflict.' Not in cold unconcern, but in flaming wrath against the foe, Jesus smites in our behalf.[1]

The second truth which Tim perceived in the story was that if some preachers are to be believed, Jesus made a mistake. If all we are to live for on earth is to get to heaven, why did he not leave Lazarus in the comfort of the grave? Instead, he pulled him back from the glory of God's presence to share the sorrows and heartaches of life on earth again. The fact that he waited four days only underlined the point. According to the Jewish tradition of the time, a person's spirit left the body on the fourth day. Lazarus was well and truly dead to the world.

When Jesus claimed to be 'the resurrection and the life', and then called the mummified corpse to stagger from the tomb, he was saying three things about himself, Tim realised. First, that he is the author and sustainer of creation; 'he is affirming the worth of living in this world'. Secondly, that he gives new life to those who are spiritually dead in their sins. And thirdly that he promises and gives life after death. 'We must never put the truth of heaven in such a way that makes this life meaningless.'

Joining those two truths together – Jesus's anger and his affirmation of earthly life – gives some guidance about how to face suffering. The Christian does not succumb in the quiet acquiescence born of a religion based on fatalism; what will be, will be. Rather, he is challenged to fight the suffering and its cause. The Spirit who inspired the social reformers leads his people still in the continued fight against all forms of evil.

'Where there's hope, fight. In my situation you fight like mad; there's something unnatural about being cut down in the prime of life.' That determination drove Tim through his leukaemia experience; having latched on to the truth he would not let go of it. The single-mindedness which evidenced itself in the immature passions of a lanky schoolboy and vocal student stayed with him into maturity to become a life-line in suffering. 'I never gave up the will to live.'

The Christian does not grasp such truths in desperation, however; they are much more than straws to cling to in the face of hopeless despair. This life is important, but it is not all there is. 'There may come a time to say enough is enough. At the point when I really understand that the fight has been lost then I'll welcome the opportunity to meet God face to face, and to become part of a new order where peace and justice exist.'

We are to fight the evils of the world with all the weapons we have – weapons of human knowledge and of spiritual warfare – until God in his all-knowing kingship decides that the time has come for us to lay down our arms. We may sometimes find the timing of his decisions strange; one day we shall know that they were right.

Twice in particular Tim has had to face the real possibility that he could die, however strong his conviction that, as with Lazarus, his sickness would not end in death. Once was when Hodgkin's Disease recurred after the initial remission. 'I was at the point where I was saying I am prepared to meet my maker.'

The second was when leukaemia struck. Although he had been a Christian for the best part of two decades, the possibility that he could soon be standing before the judge of all the earth focussed his attention on his own human sinfulness. 'I went through a profound sense of guilt, to the point where I was almost unable to forgive myself.' But the essence of Christian faith is that through the death of Jesus Christ those who seek God's forgiveness will receive it. The assurance was renewed as he searched and prayed: 'I knew that God had really forgiven me.'

With that kind of spiritual preparation, death itself held no horrors for him, although he recognised that the same might not hold true if he faced it a third time. 'Death is something the Christian needn't fear, although some do. Perhaps that's because of an inadequate understanding of what's beyond it.'

Death may be an evil thing, an intruder into the party whose presence casts a sombre shadow over it, but God has transformed it into the gateway to his presence. And so death, the ultimate blasphemy, becomes the ultimate healing – the healing everyone needs even if they are physically and mentally fit to the end of their days. The mortal has to put on the immortal, and frail flesh will be relieved of all its woes.

Heaven is sometimes thought of as a lavish eventide home where angelic servants glide serenely to wait on the guests' every need. Or even as a prolonged worship service which achieves what on earth has always proved impossible: a style which suits everyone. The Bible, however, talks about 'a new heaven and a new earth' – a new creation which in some unimaginable way will be without blemish and yet gather together and renew all that was right and good in earthly life. Jesus reconciled 'all things' on earth and in heaven 'by making peace through his blood, shed on the cross' (Col. 1:20).

For Tim, that means 'there'll be new things to learn and enjoy. There will be creative problems to solve. Will Bach be able to play around with a Yamaha organ – or will we be able to play his music on the instruments he wrote it for? We'll still be making and doing things. We'll be able to talk with the Lord about the issues which puzzled us, and there'll be no sense of possessiveness about the time others spend with him. And I can't imagine it without food – or the equivalent enjoyment to good food and drink!' Hugh Sylvester, who himself died a premature death from cancer, expressed such a hope thus:

> The main point is, we shall be satisfied. We shall never be able to think *all* God's thoughts after Him, for you would have to *be* God in order to do that. But from our standpoint as creatures . . . we shall see as much of the eternal dance as we are able and in that viewing will find delight and an appreciation of which our present theatre-going is a parody. Nor shall we be mere spectators, for the dance

will not be complete without us.[2]

To die is not to fail. Those who are not healed of their earthly ills are but the early arrivals who have gone on ahead to God's banquet before the rest of us. Our turn to enter shall come, and whether it shall follow illness or accident, or happen after the mere flicker of an eyelid, is God's business. We can be certain that it shall not be a moment too soon.

The fact of leaving this world raises all kinds of practical problems, if it is not to cause needless headaches for those who are left behind. In 1973 Tim had virtually no material wealth; he lived in rented accommodation and possessed only a few clothes and books. In 1985 he had a house bought with a mortgage, and the paraphernalia which goes with it. The low cost endowment mortgage would have been paid off automatically if he died, but he had made no will.

As soon as the diagnosis was announced, he called a friend who was a solicitor in Guildford and asked him to come round and draw up a will. It was too late by then, of course, to take out any additional life insurance, but as neither he nor Margaret believed in tying their money up for future uncertainties they did not lose any sleep over that one. Having no children, and with Margaret working, their need was rather less than for some other families.

All the household documents were scattered in different places. To make life easier for Margaret in the event of his death, Tim bought a small metal filing cabinet and put everything together. The funeral details he wrote out for Margaret: the hymns he wanted, the people who should be involved. He had a slight preference for burial rather than cremation ('I would like a place where Margaret knows I am buried'); they can see a cemetery from their bedroom window.

He did not always find that the hospital way of death was as open and down to earth as his own, especially during his earlier stay with Hodgkin's Disease. Once, he saw someone go into the lavatory and stay there for over half an hour. Tim went into the next cubicle but could hear no sound of life. He told a nurse, 'I think he's dead.' The staff broke in and found that the man had indeed died. Yet the curtains were pulled round Tim's bed to prevent him from seeing the mortuary trolley (a theatre trolley with a coffin slung beneath it and disguised by a sheet draped over the sides).

Enquiries about patients known to have died were met with vague euphemisms: 'He's gone out'; 'he's been moved'. Attitudes had changed considerably by 1985. On one occasion a nurse, with tears in her eyes, told Tim that one of his fellow patients had died – although that was still an exceptional break with protocol.

An official cover-up may be understandable; the medical profession is in the business of saving life, not losing it. But to deny the fact that death happens (and not because the doctors have 'failed'), to deny that it is, in Bernard Shaw's phrase, the ultimate statistic ('one out of one dies'), can be counter-productive. 'If you keep removing death from people, if you keep them in a totally sanitised environment, how are they ever going to come to terms with their own mortality?'

The fact of death cannot be completely hidden, and Tim watched men die in the wards. Quite apart from reminding him of his own mortality, it raised another issue. 'People think that death is the worst thing that can happen. I think the worst thing is people dying without Christ.'

At art college, he had not been reticent about sharing his faith, nor about raising the subject. At UCCF, he had been paid to talk about life before and after death. At the BBC he had encouraged religious matters to be aired in normally non-religious slots. At *Third Way* he was actively encouraging Christians to go into the world with a whole gospel, which recognised man's physical, intellectual, emotional, cultural, social, moral and spiritual dimensions.

So was the cancer patient to turn evangelist on the ward, taking as part of God's purpose in him being there the opportunity it gave him to speak to men about spiritual truths? There could have been no public doubts about where his loyalties lay during either illness. When he was well enough to go out on Sundays, he went to church and most people would know where he was going. Besides, he could hardly keep his occupation a secret (when he had one), and that spoke for itself. He had two specific opportunities to think out what he should do as he watched fellow patients take their final and irreversible steps towards the grave.

In 1973 an old man, withered and yellow, lay dying in the bed opposite Tim when he was on the main Greenhow Ward after the operation to remove his spleen. The man's son came in each night and sat by the bed. So far as Tim knew, the man had no personal hope in Christ. He was probably eighty years old. What had filled those long, now hidden years? The pleasures of family life and the pains of two world wars; the drudgery of work and the gossip of pub and club? He might have been a scoundrel or a saint; he was probably a mixture of both. Only God knew his full history.

Had God been silent all those years? Had the Hound of Heaven never even whelped, let alone pursued? Surely he is never totally silent, never completely still; only self-imposed spiritual deafness or blindness can shut out the reminders of his existence and the claims of his love. 'I couldn't say that God hadn't given him a chance. Why do we think that *the* chance comes just before death?'

The old man's last hours in hospital may not, in fact, have been the most crucial in his life. He may have made his decision already and was prepared to die with it. He was in any case so ill that he was incapable of taking in any further information or ideas; perhaps of making any decision at all. He was on his own with what he had accumulated over the years.

Tim reckoned that it would be insensitive to bound up to him and enquire after his soul. But he would, and did, pray for him. He prayed that God's justice would be done in the man's life – the justice which had held out its loving hand to him and which was sensitive enough to gauge the faintest response from him. If he had never heard the gospel once in eighty years what had the churches been doing? The responsibility for the old man's eternal destiny did not lie entirely – if at all – on Tim's shoulders, which were themselves bowed with pain and disease.

If God is in control at all, then he was in control of that man's life too. 'My prayer was a way of praying through my own discussion with God.' The night he thought the issue through and prayed his prayer for justice, the old man died.

The second occasion Tim faced the issue was in 1985; in some respects it made a greater impact on him. 'You are still thinking a lot about death because of your new friend,' Margaret noted after one visit in May, when Tim was again on the main ward during the consolidation course of chemotherapy.

His 'new friend' was a Syrian doctor who had Advanced Hodgkin's Disease. He had been treated with all four known regimes of chemotherapy. All had failed. He was mobile and mentally alert, but he knew that he would die soon. He was, Tim assumed, a nominal Muslim. Their relationship had begun simply enough. The Syrian walked past Tim's bed, and the ever-friendly leukaemia patient said, 'Hello'.

They spent a lot of time talking after that. The Syrian had faced additional burdens to Tim; his wife had refused to accept that he had cancer. On his first hospital stay she had even refused to visit him, and when he went home between treatments she expected him to live a full life at once. Now she could not hide the fact of his illness from herself any longer, she had started drinking heavily.

Again, Tim prayed, this time for a clear opportunity to speak about the hope that is in Christ, and he waited expectantly for the opportunity to come. It never did. He had made himself available to God, but for reasons which were beyond him his help had not been required.

His conclusion, that hospital bedsides and the closing hours of a person's life may not always be the appropriate circumstances for evangelism, was confirmed by the experience of Margaret's father. Once when he drove her into London to see Tim in isolation he wore his clerical collar and used the two hours he had to spare by 'visiting' the other patients in the ward. He found little more interest in spiritual things than if he had been knocking on doors down a street in his parish.

Eleventh hour repentance does happen, and Jesus's acceptance of the penitent thief on the cross beside him shows that it can also be valid. However, leading others to faith is much more a matter for the whole Church than it is for any one individual. Relationships have to be built between Church members and non-Christians in the context of loving concern and long-term friendship; only then is there usually a sufficient foundation for the right individual, who is in the right place at the right time, to build on by his or her timely words.

There is more to Christian ministry than just talking, of course, just as there is more to life than conversation. The person who has suffered may be better placed than others to assist people who are in need. There were times when Tim provided a listening ear, a soothing voice or a helping hand which the hospital staff, however caring, could not provide. He knew suffering at first-hand and could identify with what others felt. Once, as he arrived for treatment, a doctor pointed out a new patient who was very depressed and asked Tim to talk to him.

When a newly qualified doctor came to the ward to give Tim platelets the patient became the labourer and helped him to connect the bags to the drip. Knowing that a man in the ward needed the same treatment he volunteered to help again; the job was easier with two pairs of hands. Later, when the same man was distressed, needing more platelets because he was bleeding but having to wait a long time to get them, Tim was able to offer some reassurance.

But all the preparation in the world, spiritual and material, could never remove all the pain of death. As Tim contemplated his own possible demise and watched others die too, what hurt him as much as angered him was the knowledge that Margaret would grieve. He had no desire to cause her pain. 'I found it hard to imagine Margaret at my funeral. It was the dominant worst image. I don't want that pain for anyone.'

At one point she herself was unsure whether, as a Christian, she should grieve. Would that not be rather selfish, thinking only of her own loss? But if Jesus wept, so may we. Tim reassured her that the very nature of their close relationship made grief at a partner's loss natural and even proper. No love can accept such a violent and irreversible separation without being cut to the depths. No man is an island; the death of one person sends out emotional shock waves, like an earth tremor, to people some distance from the epicentre.

But there is something for the Christian to look forward to: release from evil, sin and pain, and entry into the new, perfect creation of God. 'Joy is the qualifier of grief. Grief is always temporary, joy is eternal. We know we are going to die. There is joy when we come to terms with our own mortality.' And that is not just when people are reunited in heaven; there can be a trace of it now.

Tim and Margaret had grown fond of Delia Smith's cookery books. The evening after the 'writing on the wall speech' from David Linch, revealing Tim's almost unique monocytic condition, he and Margaret sat watching a BBC TV trailer for Delia Smith's new TV series (and book) *One is fun!* Tim turned to Margaret and said, 'I know what to buy you if I'm going to die!' They fell about laughing – and he bought her the book.

He who can face eternity with faith-full laughter can face life with fresh zeal.

Tim was in hospital with septicaemia, after the Greenbelt Festival. Within three days it had cleared sufficiently for him to go home. On the following Sunday morning, 1 September, he was fit enough to bring to the congregation of Emmanuel, Stoughton, his insights into life and death based on the story of the raising of Lazarus.

It would have made a neat end to the narrative of his suffering. But it was not quite over yet.

Twenty-Two

Back to the future

A week after he had preached on the raising of Lazarus, Tim was unwell yet again. His neck felt tender, and spasms of pain were shooting through it. He phoned the hospital, and a Registrar agreed that he should ask a local doctor to look at him. There was clearly something wrong, but there was no reason for him to go to hospital. Tim was quite sure that it was not Hodgkin's Disease making a late reappearance.

When he became feverish, however, he had to go in to the Middlesex. It was early Sunday evening, and he asked a neighbour with a large estate car to drive him in; they put a foam mattress in the back and Tim lay on it for the journey. He almost fell into bed when he got there; his temperature topped 103°F and he developed rigors. The massive infection, the doctors decided, had probably gained illegal entry through the Hickman Line; they took it out. To get drugs into his body, they inserted a tube into his arm, but after a while the vein went hard and that route closed down.

Because he needed more drugs, the doctors had to insert a new temporary 'CVP' line into him. The thought of another minor operation to insert a line was too much. He broke down. A group of doctors at his bedside immediately walked away, leaving only the Consultant David Linch and Registrar Steve Schey with him, a sensitive gesture which the patient appreciated.

The line was inserted with a local anaesthetic in the intensive care unit. While he was there, a doctor visiting the hospital came to look round. He spoke with a Dutch accent, and proved to be a valuable distraction for Tim. The first *Third Way* lecture was due to be given at the end of September – by a Dutchman, Bob Goudzwaard (pronounced as if the first letter were an H). He was a professor of economics in Amsterdam, and had been a leading light in forming the new political alliance, The Christian Democratic Appeal. Tim tried the name out on the visiting doctor, to see if he had ever heard of him, and he had. Talking to the Dutchman about the Netherlands was a bright spot in an otherwise drab twelve days in hospital. For the rest of the time, Tim rather uncharacteristically kept himself to himself.

He had had enough of hospital, even if he had received excellent treatment and had been introduced to the best side of the National Health Service. When he once told a ward sister that he felt he had been very privileged (meaning it in the sense that he had been well cared for), she promptly responded that he had been treated no differently to anyone else. He had, of course, done all he could to prevent himself from becoming completely institutionalised, and the staff had responded with willing flexibility once they knew that he could be trusted to do what he was told on the important matters. He had also been looked after by a team of people working at the frontiers of medicine, and who recognised that patients are not just slabs of meat.

With the infection cleared, he was able to return to normal life again. And it was normal: the monocytic condition had been corrected. The treatment had been effective. Not once, but twice, Tim had walked away from the scourge of cancer.

The return to normality had its moments, though. The process of readjustment came harder to both Tim and Margaret than either had expected. It was not simply a matter of picking up life's threads where they had been hastily laid down; they had to put some extra work into their relationship.

Margaret had become used to being virtually single

again, organising her own life, making decisions alone, and even at times thinking that she might be widowed and left alone permanently. Tim's experience of suffering had been an essentially individual thing which could not be greatly shared. And because he had been starved of normal home life for months, he charged back into it with even more enthusiasm than usual. They had been together in the illness, yet they had been apart; they had walked through it together, and yet had moved at different speeds. They had to learn – gladly – to live harmoniously together again.

And to live without the prospect of children. Any hopes they may have had about adopting a multi-national family had probably been dashed for good. Tim's poor health record would make him a faller at the first fence in the necessarily long and demanding steeplechase through the adoption procedures.

How long he would remain healthy, in view of the thrashing he had been given by the diseases and the drugs, was anybody's guess and nobody was making any. On Saturday 15 February 1986, almost a year to the day after Tim had been told he had leukaemia, he and Margaret invited their friends and relatives to join in a thanksgiving service at Emmanuel church. It was a joyous reunion for people from all periods of Tim's life. During the service, the vicar of Emmanuel, John Salter, told the 200 people present, 'Tim is with us and that's a cause for thanksgiving, and we sing praise to God with all our hearts. Whatever the future holds, no one knows. Any healing any of us has is temporary and partial. We say to God: "You are sovereign".'

Tim and Margaret had already decided how to live with uncertainty – no more uncertainty than most people face, but which in their case had been brought more obviously to their attention. Margaret: 'Experiences are to be valued for what they are, now. It's fatal to ask will we have another holiday together or will we walk through Trafalgar Square together, because that just spoils the experience at the time. I've tried to blank that out of my mind. If they happen again, well – tremendous! If they don't, at least I'll have enjoyed the last one!'

Tim: 'I don't go around thinking I may only have a couple of years left and I must do this or that. That's a silly way to live. There are things that I'd like to do before I die, but next year there'll be more things that I'll find I want to do. There's never going to be a fixed event which, when it's done, you can say your life is complete. I have no anxiety day by day whether I live or not. I don't like the prospect of death; I don't want to die; and I've no intention whatever of dying at this stage. I'll worry about it if they tell me I've got the monocytic condition or leukaemia back again.'

That does not imply that they are in any way careless about the life which has been so remarkably restored to them. Tim came back with new perspectives. His second close encounter with death had made him more aware of the value of this world in God's purposes; and that he saw as a call to responsibility.

While he was ill, he had asked himself what he would say to his heavenly Father if he met him soon. Would he have anything to show for his thirty-five years on earth? Had it been worthwhile? He had the enforced time, which perhaps everyone should voluntarily take occasionally, to check if he was being bowled along in the wrong direction by the forceful winds of habit. He emerged with a renewed conviction that he was on the right track of God's purposes for his life. That in turn gave him a contentment which prevented as yet unfulfilled ambitions – such as making documentary films – from becoming obsessions. He determined to take more considered decisions over what he would and would not do, rather than accept every invitation to do something or be somewhere.

His almost compulsive enthusiasm for work had the edge taken off it, not by making him work-shy but by challenging his priorities so that other things would be given their rightful place in his life. One was his home. The kitchen needed renovating; that, he realised, was a matter of stewardship as well as of comfort. Having seen his temporal lifespan in the context of God's on-going and eternal purposes, he saw the temporary occupancy of bricks and mortar in the context of continuing human history. He had a responsibility to keep it in repair for the next owner, and the next generation, to enjoy.

So the Tim Dean overture continues on the note which has sounded so strongly through most of its movements since those far-off days of sixth form parties and their late night discussions: a celebration of and dedication to a Creator God who has richly endowed the earth with great treasure for his creatures to enjoy. Beautiful music, good food and drink, homes and gardens, families and friends: there are a million and one new things to learn and discover, and we shall never fully plumb the depths of even the most familiar. Life is too short for them all, which is why God has added eternity to our options.

He is God of the good times and the bad times as well; a God of life, who has conquered death; who affirms the value of this world, and is making an even better one to come.

At the thanksgiving service, the congregation sang Bishop Timothy Dudley-Smith's hymn *Lord for the years*. It begins with a highly appropriate glance at the past, and especially at God's faithfulness in the details:

> Lord, for the years your love has kept and guided,
> urged and inspired us, cheered us on our way,
> sought us and saved us, pardoned and provided:
> Lord of the years, we bring our thanks today.

It ends with abandonment to Christ, come what may in the uncertain future:

> Lord for ourselves; in living power remake us –
> self on the cross and Christ upon the throne,
> past put behind us, for the future take us:
> Lord of our lives, to live for Christ alone.

You do not need to have fought off the greedy advances of death twice in your life before you can sing it. But the fact that a thirty-five year old man has thus fought, has come back to tell the tale, and can still sing both verses with all his heart, says as much about the truth and challenge of the words for Everyman as it says about Tim Dean.

'The fact that I have had cancer doesn't shake my belief that God is a God of love and justice. Why should it? I have a theology that gives some kind of framework to why there's suffering in the world. I have confidence that if I ache, God aches even more, that it will work out to his glory, and that part of his answer is what I do as one of his ambassadors.

'The Christian difference in suffering is not the ex-pectation of healing; it is just this, that I know whether I shall live a normal life or eventually go to the grave with leukaemia, that Christ will be with me all the time, and if necessary walk with me to the grave.'

Afterword

Tim Dean

There is only so much that can be said in a book. To mention every person who played a role in the story, would add a plethora of names that could only frustrate the reader. So for the sake of clarity and the relief of tedium many people, some very close to Margaret and myself, who have played a crucial part in this saga, are never mentioned. It would not be appropriate to name them individually, and to thank them all in the last page or two of this volume, other than to offer a general heart-felt 'thank-you' to all who have loved and cared for us. It is particularly important to thank all those, possibly including yourself, who have remembered faithfully in prayer while never having met us, and who remain anonymous to us.

I would however like to mention one group of people: those who, however temporarily, became good friends around my bedside in hospital. Many student nurses came and went whose names I never will remember, what I won't forget is their care, patience and when I was up to it, ability to inject some fun into the isolation. 'Thank you' always seems to be such a tame way to express deep felt gratitude to people who continually showed greater care and interest than one would normally expect from strangers or people outside one's circle of friends and acquaintances. But I would like to acknowledge here my thanks to these particular people: Dr David Linch, Dr Steve Schey (now a consultant at Guy's Hospital), Sister Beverley Cornish, Dr Michael Marber, and also those I have known much longer, Dr Jelliffe and Dr Gillian Vaughan Hudson (now director of the British Lymphoma Investigation). My thanks also go to their colleagues: Sam Machin, Hannah Cohen, Libby Macintyre, David Cummins, Sally Kinsey, Sister Lowe, Marilyn Marks, Sue Evans, Anne Yardumian, Pip Morton, Nicky Ronayne, Helen Wilson, and not least Henri.

One person from the hospital deserves special mention, Dr Allison Brownell. A member of the Haematology team that was to treat me for leukemia, Alison and her husband Ken have been personal friends for many years. I was especially grateful for her friendship during those weeks in isolation, in a situation which could not have been easy.

Lastly, my thanks go to Derek Williams who has not only played a part in this story, but spent many hours dredging through the mire of my past. Whatever perverse form of masochism possessed you?

UNDER THE SHADOW

The video referred to on page 138 has been produced by Angela Keith for Scripture Union. *Under the Shadow* is a series of three programmes on themes related to Easter. The programme *The Sharp Edge* Tim and Margaret Dean. It can be purchased from SU Bookshops, and is also available for hire from SU Mail Order, PO Box 38, Bristol BS99 7NA.

HODGKIN'S DISEASE ASSOCIATION

A patient and family self-help charity to give advice and support to people affected by Hodgkin's disease and Non-Hodgkin's Lymphoma has been set up by a number of people including Tim Dean.

Further information: Hodgkin's Disease Association, PO Box 275, Haddenham, Aylesbury, Bucks, or phone 0844 291 500.

References

Chapter Four

1 Rookmaaker, H. R., *Modern Art and the death of a culture*, IVP 1971, p. 136

Chapter Ten

1 *Third Way*, December 1984.
2 Wenham, John. *The Goodness of God*, IVP 1974, p. 70 (Subsequently re-issued as *The Enigma of Evil*).

Chapter Twelve

1 Packer, J. I., *Evangelism and the sovereignty of God*, IVP 1963, p. 22f.

Chapter Thirteen

1 Lewis, C. S., *The Problem of Pain*, Bles 1950, p. 81.

Chapter Fourteen

1 Information about *Third Way* can be obtained from Elm House, 37 Elm Road, New Malden, Surrey, KT3 3HB.

2 *Third Way*, December 1985.

Chapter Seventeen

1 *Third Way*, December 1985.

Chapter Twenty

1 The three 'Third Way Books' published by SPCK in 1985 were: Lyon, David, *The steeple's shadow* (on secularisation); Storkey, Elaine, *What's right with feminism*; and Walter, Tony. *All you love is need* (on a contemporary attitude which has assumed the proportions of a substitute religion).

Chapter Twenty-One

1 Warfield, B. B., *The person and work of Christ*, p. 116, quoted by R.V.G. Tasker in *The Gospel according to John*, IVP (Tyndale Commentary) 1979, p. 140.
2 Sylvester, Hugh, *Arguing with God*, IVP 1971, p. 123.